150 desserts
for special treats

150 desserts
for special treats

Deliciously irresistible recipes to indulge in once in a while, from coffee profiteroles to dark chocolate ice cream and from soufflés to praline pavlovas – every recipe described step-by-step and illustrated with 200 delectable colour photographs

Edited by Ann Kay

southwater

This edition is published by Southwater, an imprint of Anness Publishing Ltd, Hermes House, 88–89 Blackfriars Road, London SE1 8HA; tel. 020 7401 2077; fax 020 7633 9499

www.southwaterbooks.com; www.annesspublishing.com

If you like the images in this book and would like to investigate using them for publishing, promotions or advertising, please visit our website www.practicalpictures.com for more information.

UK agent: The Manning Partnership Ltd; tel. 01225 478444; fax 01225 478440; sales@manning-partnership.co.uk

UK distributor: Grantham Book Services Ltd; tel. 01476 541080; fax 01476 541061; orders@gbs.tbs-ltd.co.uk

North American agent/distributor: National Book Network; tel. 301 459 3366; fax 301 429 5746; www.nbnbooks.com

Australian agent/distributor: Pan Macmillan Australia; tel. 1300 135 113; fax 1300 135 103; customer.service@macmillan.com.au

New Zealand agent/distributor: David Bateman Ltd; tel. (09) 415 7664; fax (09) 415 8892

Publisher: Joanna Lorenz
Editorial Director: Helen Sudell
Editors: Ann Kay and Elizabeth Woodland
Copy-editor: Julia Canning
Design: Diane Pullen and Design Principals
Cover Design: Adelle Morris
Production Controller: Claire Rae

Previously published as part of a larger volume, *500 Desserts*

Main front cover image shows Chocolate & Chestnut Pots – for recipe, see page 62

Ethical Trading Policy

At Anness Publishing we believe that business should be conducted in an ethical and ecologically sustainable way, with respect for the environment and a proper regard to the replacement of the natural resources we employ.

As a publisher, we use a lot of wood pulp to make high-quality paper for printing, and that wood commonly comes from spruce trees. We are therefore currently growing more than 500,000 trees in two Scottish forest plantations near Aberdeen – Berrymoss (130 hectares/320 acres) and West Touxhill (125 hectares/305 acres). The forests we manage contain twice the number of trees employed each year in paper-making for our books.

Because of this ongoing ecological investment programme, you, as our customer, can have the pleasure and reassurance of knowing that a tree is being cultivated on your behalf to naturally replace the materials used to make the book you are holding.

Our forestry programme is run in accordance with the UK Woodland Assurance Scheme (UKWAS) and will be certified by the internationally recognized Forest Stewardship Council (FSC). The FSC is a non-government organization dedicated to promoting responsible management of the world's forests. Certification ensures forests are managed in an environmentally sustainable and socially responsible basis. For further information about this scheme, go to www.annesspublishing.com/trees

Notes

Bracketed terms are intended for American readers.
For all recipes, quantities are given in both metric and imperial measures and, where appropriate, in standard cups and spoons. Follow one set of measures, but not a mixture, because they are not interchangeable.
Standard spoon and cup measures are level.
1 tsp = 5ml, 1 tbsp = 15ml, 1 cup = 250ml/8fl oz.
Australian standard tablespoons are 20ml. Australian readers should use 3 tsp in place of 1 tbsp for measuring small quantities.
American pints are 16fl oz/2 cups. American readers should use 20fl oz/2.5 cups in place of 1 pint when measuring liquids.
Electric oven temperatures in this book are for conventional ovens. When using a fan oven, the temperature will probably need to be reduced by about 10–20°C/20–40°F. Since ovens vary, you should check with your manufacturer's instruction book for guidance.
The nutritional analysis given for each recipe is calculated per portion (i.e. serving or item), unless otherwise stated. If the recipe gives a range, such as Serves 4–6, then the nutritional analysis will be for the smaller portion size, i.e. 6 servings. Measurements for sodium do not include salt added to taste.
Medium (US large) eggs are used unless otherwise stated.

Important: pregnant women, the elderly, the ill and very young children should avoid recipes using raw or lightly cooked eggs.

Contents

Introduction

Desserts are always popular, whether they are sumptuous creations or the simplest of dishes. Indeed, a well-chosen dessert is guaranteed to round off a meal on a high note and can turn

even the most ordinary meal into a memorable occasion. As a finale, a mouthwatering fruit tart, a delicately flavoured ice cream or a luxurious chocolate treat will delight guests and give you, the cook, great satisfaction.

Whether you are planning an elaborate dinner party or an everyday family meal, the key to success is to make sure that the dessert you select balances perfectly with the main course. If you are serving a filling or rich main course you will need to choose a delicate or fruity option to follow, while you can afford to indulge in a rich, creamy dessert if you opt for a light main dish. With the fantastic selection of recipes featured in this book, you will never be at a loss for ideas to create a perfectly balanced menu.

The other factors that might affect your choice of dessert, such as seasonal availability and the amount of time you have for preparation, are also catered for in this collection. Many of the desserts can be made a day or two in advance, others can be started early in the day and finished off just before you eat, while frozen desserts and ice creams can be made weeks in advance, ready to serve whenever you need them. When entertaining, the more preparation

you can do ahead, the better, as this means that you will have time to enjoy the meal as much as your guests. However, there's also a wide choice of quick-to-make recipes that can be rustled up in a matter of minutes. In addition, whatever the season, you'll find a recipe to suit the time of year, and with the wide variety of tropical ingredients now available in the stores, there's a range of exciting dishes that will add an exotic flavour to your meals.

As a back-up to the recipes in this book, the introductory pages provide helpful information on preparing and baking pastry for pies and tarts, plus an invaluable guide to preparing fruit, from making perfect orange segments to creating delicate decorations. There are also ideas for easy sweet sauces to help you whip up instant desserts, plus clever presentation methods that will help you to achieve professional finishing touches. All the recipes in this book have clear, step-by-step instructions, so that even dishes that are commonly regarded as tricky, such as soufflés and roulades, are easy to make and will look and taste delicious. The important thing is to read the whole recipe through before you start, so that you understand all the steps involved and can plan the preparation properly. A large number of recipes have helpful Cook's Tips and Variations boxes, offering advice on specific aspects of a dish or interesting alternatives to get your imagination going, or to help out when you don't necessarily have all the specified ingredients to hand.

The four recipe chapters feature over 150 tempting dishes, grouped under mouthwatering categories such as Ice Cream & Cold Desserts, Hot Delights, Super Indulgent Treats and International Flavours. You will discover a wonderful selection of popular classics that feature alongside more unusual recipes that are destined to become new family favourites.

Have fun leafing through these pages at any time of year and for any occasion. For summer days you can't go wrong with a cooling Coconut & Lemon Grass Ice Cream or a simple Lemon Sorbet, while Baked Rice Pudding or divine Chocolate & Orange Scotch Pancakes are warming and tasty choices for winter. Instant entertaining is provided by Strawberry Cream Shortbreads or Baked Apples in Honey & Lemon, but to pull out all the stops impress guests with the unusual Iced Strawberry & Lemon Gâteau. International classics range from French Chocolate Soufflés to Australian Hazelnut Pavlova, including baked delights from Classic Crème Brûlée to Middle Eastern Pestiños. Whether you are a novice cook, an experienced chef, in a hurry, on a budget, preparing a mid-week family meal or catering for a lavish or important event, this superb collection of desserts will provide all the answers, and indulge every taste.

Working with Pastry

Making your own pastry may seem daunting at first, but if you follow a few basic rules and stick to the right quantities, you will soon find the technique easy. The key is not to hurry and to keep your hands cool when handling the dough. The crisp, light results are always worth the effort and the popularity of your home-made tarts and pies will be truly satisfying.

SHORTCRUST PASTRY

With shortcrust pastry and its variations, once the dough has been formed into a ball, it is usually chilled for about 20 minutes to make handling easier. After the pastry has been rolled out and used to line a tin (pan), it should be chilled again to minimize shrinkage during baking. A filled tart or pie needs only about 30 minutes otherwise the pastry will turn soggy. An empty shell, prior to blind baking, can be chilled for longer.

Heating the Oven

Whatever type of pastry you are baking, always allow time to preheat the oven; it will take about 15 minutes to reach the required temperature (fan ovens may heat more quickly). If you are baking blind or cooking a double-crust pie, it's a good idea to put a heavy baking sheet in the oven to heat up. The hot baking sheet will give the base of the pie an initial blast of heat to help keep the base crisp. It will also make it easier to slide the dish in and out of the oven.

Baking Shortcrust Pastry

Shortcrust pastries are usually baked at 200°C/400°F/Gas 6, but the temperature is often reduced part-way through baking to allow the filling to cook sufficiently. As a general rule, bake pastry in the middle of the oven, or just above the middle, unless the recipe tells you otherwise. Take care with pastries that contain added sugar; they should be removed from the oven as soon as they are golden, because they can burn quickly at this stage.

Baking Rules

When following a recipe, baking times may vary slightly depending on your oven and how chilled the pie was before cooking. Always check the pie at least 5 minutes before the end of the suggested cooking time. Don't keep opening the oven door though, or the temperature will drop and the pastry will not be as crisp. Avoid cooking the pastry with other foods that release a lot of steam as this also prevents a crisp result.

Baking Blind

This process is used for a number of reasons. It is used to partly cook an empty pastry case so that it does not become soggy when the filling is added and the final baking is done. It is also used to completely bake a pastry case when the filling cooks in a relatively short time and you need to ensure that the pastry is fully cooked through. The process is also required when the pastry case is to contain a precooked mixture or an uncooked filling. Lining the pastry case with baking parchment or foil and filling it with baking beans stops the pastry from rising up during cooking.

1 Cut out a round of baking parchment or foil about 7.5cm/3in larger than the flan tin (tart pan). Prick the base of the pastry all over with a fork.

2 Lay the baking parchment or foil in the pastry case and press it smoothly over the base and up the side.

3 Put either the commercially made ceramic baking beans, or dried beans or peas, in the case, spreading them out evenly to cover the base. Whichever kind you choose, they can be used over and over again.

4 To partially bake the pastry, bake in an oven preheated to 200°C/400°F/Gas 6 for 15 minutes, or until the pastry is set and the rim is dry and golden. Remove and lift out the paper and beans. Return the case to the oven for a further 5 minutes. The pastry case can now be filled and the baking completed.

5 For fully baked pastry, bake the case at 200°C/400°F/Gas 6 for 15 minutes, then remove the paper and beans and return to the oven. Bake for a further 5–10 minutes, or until golden brown. Cool completely before filling.

6 To bake tartlets, bake blind in the same way as flans, but allow only 6–8 minutes for partial baking, and 12–15 minutes for fully baked pastry.

Cook's Tip

Fully baked pastry cases, both large and small, may be baked up to two days ahead if carefully stored in airtight containers. Interleave them with greaseproof (waxed) paper, or use baking parchment, if you are keeping several, and always make sure that they are cooled before storing.

Cook's Tips

• *When moving rolled-out pastry dough to line a tin (pan) or dish or top a pie, roll the dough loosely around the rolling pin, lift up, then carefully unroll it on top of the container. Press gently in place.*

• *If you find any small holes in a cooked pastry case, repair them by brushing with a little beaten egg, then return the case to the oven for 2–3 minutes to seal. Any larger holes or tears that appear during baking should be repaired by pressing a little raw pastry in the gap, brushing with beaten egg, and then returning to the oven.*

• *If the pastry starts to bubble up during baking, remove from the oven, prick again with a fork to allow the trapped air to escape and return to the oven. If it has bubbled up when you take it out after cooking, don't try to press it flat, or you will crack the pastry. Make a very small slit in the case with a knife and leave it to shrink back on its own.*

• *If the pastry becomes fully browned before the filling has cooked through completely, then you should protect it by covering with foil. Cover single- or double-crust pies completely, but make a hole in the top of the foil to allow the steam to escape. When baking open flans, cover the pastry edge only – by using strips of foil.*

PUFF PASTRY

The baking method for puff, rough puff and flaky pastry has much in common with that used for shortcrust. Chilling the pastry before baking is essential, and shaped puff pastries should be chilled for at least an hour to prevent the pastry becoming mis-shapen during baking. Take great care when brushing the pastry with egg glaze; any that runs down the sides of the pastry will make the layers stick together and prevent the pastry from rising well and evenly.

Oven Temperature

This type of pastry must be cooked in a preheated hot oven, so that the air trapped within the layers expands and lifts up the pastry. If the oven is too cool, the butter will melt before the dough has a chance to cook, and the pastry will not rise well. The oven temperature is usually 230°C/450°F/Gas 8, but small pastries are sometimes cooked at 220°C/425°F/Gas 7. Reduce the temperature after about 15 minutes, to give the filling time to cook through.

Releasing Steam

When baking puff pastry pies, up to three slits or holes (depending how moist the filling is) should be made in the pastry top to allow the steam from the filling to escape. Don't make too many steam holes though, or too much air will be lost and the pastry won't rise well. After baking, cover steam holes with cooked pastry decorations.

Unlike shortcrust pastries, a steamy atmosphere helps the puff pastry to rise. Put a dish of hot water on the lowest shelf when preheating the oven. Remove it for the last few minutes of cooking. If the pastry starts to sink after cooking, it hasn't cooked sufficiently and should be returned to the oven for a little longer.

FILO PASTRY

Unlike shortcrust and puff pastries, filo pastry does not require chilling before baking. The most important point to remember is that filo must never dry out, or it will become brittle and hard to fold and shape. Keep the sheets you are not working with covered with a damp dish towel. It may also crumble if it is too cold so, before using, remove the unopened packet from the refrigerator and allow to stand for 1 hour.

Filo must always be lightly brushed with melted butter before baking to give it a shiny glaze; unsalted (sweet) butter is ideal because it has a lower water content than ordinary butter, or oil can also be used. Choose a mild-flavoured oil when making sweet pastries as you do not want the flavour of the oil to overpower delicate tastes. Be careful not to overdo the melted fat; it should be brushed as thinly and evenly as possible to create light crisp layers. Never brush filo with egg or milk as this would make it soggy.

Oven Temperature

The usual temperature for baking filo pastry is 200°C/400°F/Gas 6, although it can be cooked at a slightly lower temperature without its crisp texture being affected. Filo pastry colours very quickly, so always check frequently towards the end of the cooking time. If the pastry has browned sufficiently before the filling is cooked, cover it loosely with foil, then remove again for the last few minutes to make sure the top of the pie is dry and crisp.

Leftover Filo Pastry

Wrap any unused filo in clear film (plastic wrap) and return it to the refrigerator. It will keep for seven to ten days. It is possible to re-freeze filo, but don't do this more than once.

Preparing Fruit

Fresh fruit provides the perfect base for all manner of delicious and healthy desserts. To make the most of the different types of fruit, there are certain preparation techniques that will always be useful, whether you are making a fresh fruit salad or creating a more elaborate dessert. For professional results, just follow the step instructions below.

BUYING FRUIT

Obviously, the best time to buy fruit is when it is fully ripe and at its peak. The exceptions are fruits such as bananas and pears, which ripen quickly and can therefore be bought in an under-ripe condition and allowed to ripen fully at home. You are most likely to find top-quality fruits in markets and shops that have a quick turnover of fresh produce, preferably with a daily delivery. Although most fruits are now available almost all the year round, they are nearly always best and cheapest when in season in the country of origin. Only buy as much fruit as you need at one time so that it remains fresh and appetizing.

PREPARING FRUIT

For some fruits, the only preparation needed is washing or wiping with a damp cloth; others must be peeled, cored, stoned (pitted) or seeded. Wash fruit only just before using. If necessary, cut away any bruised or damaged parts.

Peeling Firm Fruit

Some firm fruits, such as eating apples and pears, can be served raw without peeling. For cooking, peeling is often necessary. Pare off the skin as thinly as possible to avoid losing the valuable nutrients under the skin.

1 To peel fruit, first wash it and then pat it dry by using kitchen paper. Use a small, sharp paring knife or a vegetable peeler to pare off the skin in long, thin vertical strips all round the fruit, making sure that you cut into the fruit as thinly as possible. Pears in particular are best peeled by this method.

2 Alternatively, for apples, thinly peel all round the fruit in a spiral.

Coring Firm Fruit

1 To core whole apples and pears, place the sharp edge of a corer over the stem end of the fruit.

2 Press the corer down firmly into the fruit, and then twist it slightly; the core, complete with all of the pips (seeds), should come away in the centre of the corer. Now push out the corer from the handle end to remove the complete core cleanly.

Cook's Tips

Storage methods depend on the type of fruit, but there are some basic guidelines:
• Do not wash fruit before storing, but only when ready to use.
• Store fruit at the bottom of the refrigerator or in the salad crisper.
• Do not refrigerate unripe fruit; keep it at room temperature or in a cool, dark place, depending on the variety.
• Fragile fruits such as summer berries are easily squashed during storage, so spread them out in a single layer on a tray lined with kitchen paper.

Segmenting Firm Fruit

1 Halve the fruit lengthways, then cut into quarters or segments.

2 Now cut out the central core and pips using a small, sharp knife, taking care not to cut yourself as you work the knife towards you.

Cook's Tip

Some fruits, such as apples, pears and bananas, quickly oxidize and turn brown when exposed to the air. To prevent discoloration, brush cut fruits with lemon juice. Alternatively, acidulate a bowl of cold water by stirring in the juice of half a lemon. Drop the cut fruits into the bowl immediately after preparing.

Peeling Citrus Fruit

It is very important to remove all of the bitter white pith that lies just beneath the rind of citrus fruits.

1 To peel firm-skinned fruits, hold the fruit over a bowl to catch the juice and use a sharp knife to cut off the rind.

2 Alternatively, cut a slice off the top and bottom of the fruit, place on a board and, cutting downwards, slice off the rind in strips,

3 For loose-skinned fruit, such as tangerines, pierce the skin with your forefinger at the stalk end and peel off the rind. Pull off all the white shreds adhering to the fruit.

Segmenting Citrus Fruit

1 Using a small serrated knife, cut down between the membranes enclosing the segments; ease out the flesh.

Grating Citrus Fruit

1 For finely grated rind, grate the fruit against the fine face of a grater. Remove only the coloured rind; if you grate too deeply into the peel, you will be in danger of including the bitter white pith.

2 For thinly pared strips of rind, use a cannelle knife (zester) or vegetable peeler, then cut into shreds if necessary.

Decorating with Citrus Fruit

1 To make thick julienne strips of rind, cut lengthways, using a cannelle knife.

2 To make twists, slice the fruits thinly, cut to the centre, then twist the ends in opposite directions to make an S-shape.

Peeling Soft Fruit

Fruits such as peaches, nectarines and apricots can be peeled with a sharp paring knife, but this may waste some of the delicious flesh. It is better to loosen the skins by dipping them briefly in boiling water.

1 To remove the skins quickly and cleanly from peaches, nectarines and apricots, start by making a tiny nick in the skin, using the point of a sharp knife. This is done in order to help the skins spring off the flesh when the fruits are immersed in water. Take care when you are handling the soft fruit as the flesh can be easily damaged by clutching the fruit too firmly.

2 Cover with boiling water and leave for 15–30 seconds, depending on the ripeness of the fruit. Remove the fruit with a slotted spoon and peel off the skin, which should come away easily.

Removing Stones (Pits) and Seeds

1 Cut all round the fruit through the seam. Twist the halves in opposite directions, then lever out the stone (pit).

2 To pit cherries, simply place a cherry in a cherry stoner and then push the bar firmly into the fruit. The pit will be neatly ejected.

3 To remove the seeds from grapes, first cut the grapes in half, and then pick out the tiny pips using the tip of a small sharp knife.

4 To remove either papaya or melon seeds, you should first cut the fruit in half using a sharp knife, and then neatly scoop out all of the seeds with a spoon.

Dessert Sauces

Fresh custards and flavoured sweet white sauces are classic dessert sauces, but quick and easy dessert toppings can be made almost instantly from ready-made ingredients. These are ideal to serve over scoops of ice cream or with crêpes to create no-fuss desserts. Simple sauces can also be used imaginatively to create special finishing touches to desserts.

USING VANILLA PODS (BEANS)

Vanilla pods are often used in sweet dessert sauces – most commonly to flavour milk, cream or sugar.

Vanilla Infusions

1 To infuse (steep) vanilla flavour into milk or cream for a sauce, put the milk or cream in a pan, add the whole vanilla pod and heat gently over a low heat until almost boiling. Remove from the heat, cover and leave to stand for 10 minutes. Remove the pod, rinse and dry; it may be re-used several times.

2 To get maximum flavour, use a sharp knife to slit the pod lengthways, then open it out. Use the tip of the knife to scrape out the sticky black seeds inside: add to the hot sauce.

Vanilla Sugar

Many dessert sauces benefit from the delicate flavour of vanilla-flavoured sugar. This is available ready-made from shops but it is easy to make your own version.

1 To make vanilla sugar, simply bury a vanilla pod in a jar of white sugar. Cover tightly for a few weeks until the sugar takes on the vanilla flavour. Shake the jar occasionally.

SPEEDY SAUCES FOR TOPPING ICE CREAM

Store-cupboard (pantry) ingredients can often be transformed into irresistible sauces to spoon on top of ice cream.

Marshmallow Melt

1 Melt 90g/3½oz marshmallows with 30ml/2 tbsp milk or cream in a small pan. Add a little grated nutmeg and stir until smooth. Serve immediately.

Black Forest Sauce

1 Drain a can of black cherries, reserving the juice. Blend a little of the juice with a little arrowroot or cornflour (cornstarch).

2 Add the cornflour mixture to the rest of the juice in a pan. Stir until boiling and lightly thickened, then add the cherries and a dash of kirsch and heat through.

Raspberry Coulis

1 Purée some thawed frozen raspberries, with icing (confectioners') sugar to taste, then press through a sieve (strainer).

2 Blend a little cornflour (cornstarch) with some orange juice, and stir into the purée; cook for 2 minutes until thick. Cool.

Chocolate-Toffee Sauce

1 Chop a Mars bar and heat very gently in a pan, stirring until just melted. Spoon over scoops of vanilla ice cream and sprinkle with chopped nuts.

Marmalade Whisky Sauce

1 Heat 60ml/4 tbsp chunky marmalade in a pan with 30ml/2 tbsp whisky, until just melted. Allow to bubble for a few seconds then spoon over ice cream.

Nutty Butterscotch Sauce

1 Melt 75g/3oz/6 tbsp butter and 175g/6oz/¾ cup soft dark brown sugar in a heavy pan, then bring to the boil and boil for 2 minutes. Cool the mixture for 5 minutes.

2 Heat 175ml/6fl oz/¾ cup evaporated (unsweetened condensed) milk to just below boiling point, then gradually stir into the sugar mixture. Cook over a low heat for 2 minutes, stirring frequently.

3 Spread 50g/2oz/½ cup hazelnuts on a baking sheet and toast under a hot grill (broiler). Turn them on to a clean dish towel and rub off the skins. Chop the nuts roughly and stir into the sauce.

PRESENTATION IDEAS

When you've made a delicious sauce for a special dessert, why not make more of it by using it for decoration on the plate, too? Try one of the following simple ideas to make your sauce into a talking point. Individual slices of desserts, cakes or tarts, or a stuffed baked peach, look especially good served with sauce presented in this way.

Marbling

Use this technique when you have two contrasting sauces of a similar thickness, such as a fruit purée with cream or thin fresh custard.

1 Spoon alternate spoonfuls of the two sauces on to a serving plate or shallow dish. Using a spoon, stir the sauces lightly together, gently swirling to create a marbled effect.

Yin-Yang Sauces

This oriental pattern is ideal for two contrasting colours of purée or coulis, such as a raspberry and a mango fruit coulis. It is important to make sure that the flavours of the sauce complement one another.

1 Spoon a sauce on one side of a serving plate or shallow bowl. Add the second sauce to the other side, then gently push the two sauces together with the spoon, swirling one around the other, to make a yin-yang shape.

Drizzling

1 Pour a smooth sauce or coulis into a container or tube with a fine pouring lip.

2 Drizzle the sauce in droplets or fine wavy lines on to the plate around the area where the dessert will sit.

Piping Outlines

1 Spoon a small amount of fruit coulis or chocolate sauce into a piping (pastry) bag fitted with a plain writing nozzle.

2 Carefully pipe the outline of a simple shape on to a serving plate, then spoon in the same sauce to fill the space within the outline.

Feathering Hearts

1 Flood the plate with a smooth sauce such as chocolate sauce or fruit purée. Add small droplets of pouring cream into it at intervals.

2 Draw the tip of a small knife through the droplets of cream, to drag each drop into a heart.

QUICK SAUCES FOR CRÊPES

Give crêpes and pancakes a lift with these three easy ideas.

Rich Butterscotch Sauce

1 Heat 75g/3oz/6 tbsp butter, 175g/6oz/ ¾ cup soft light brown sugar and 30ml/ 2 tbsp golden (light corn) syrup in a pan over a low heat until melted.

2 Remove from the heat and add 75ml/5 tbsp double (heavy) cream, stirring constantly, until smooth.

Orange Caramel Sauce

1 Melt 25g/1oz/2 tbsp unsalted (sweet) butter in a heavy pan. Stir in 50g/2oz/ ¼ cup caster (superfine) sugar and cook until golden brown.

2 Add the juice of 2 oranges and ½ lemon; stir until the caramel has dissolved.

Summer Berry Sauce

1 Melt 25g/1oz/2 tbsp butter in a frying pan. Add 50g/2oz/¼ cup caster (superfine) sugar and cook until golden.

2 Add the juice of 2 oranges and the rind of ½ orange and cook until syrupy. Add 350g/12oz/3 cups mixed summer berries and warm through.

3 Add 45ml/3 tbsp orange-flavoured liqueur and set alight. Serve immediately.

Chocolate Sorbet with Red Fruits

Mouthwatering chocolate-flavoured sorbet tastes and looks stunning when served with a selection of luscious red berries.

Serves 6
475ml/16fl oz/2 cups water
45ml/3 tbsp clear honey
90g/3½oz/½ cup caster (superfine) sugar

75g/3oz/⅔ cup cocoa powder (unsweetened)
50g/2oz plain (semisweet) or dark (bittersweet) chocolate, chopped into small pieces
400g/14oz soft red fruits, such as raspberries, redcurrants or strawberries

1 Put the water in a pan with the honey, sugar and cocoa. Heat gently, stirring occasionally, until the sugar has completely dissolved.

2 Remove the pan from the heat, add the chocolate pieces and stir until melted. Leave until cool.

3 Pour the chocolate mixture into a freezer container and freeze until slushy. Whisk quickly until smooth, then return the mixture to the freezer again and freeze until almost firm. Whisk the iced mixture for a second time, cover the container and freeze until firm.

4 Alternatively, use an ice cream maker to freeze the mixture, following the manufacturer's instructions.

5 Remove the sorbet from the freezer 10–15 minutes before serving to soften slightly. Serve in scoops, in chilled dessert bowls, with the soft fruits.

Cook's Tip
Chocolate curls make an attractive decoration and are very easy to create. Simply chill a bar of chocolate, then use a vegetable peeler to shave off curls along the length of the bar.

Ginger & Kiwi Sorbet

Freshly grated root ginger gives a lively, aromatic flavour to this exotic sorbet, while the black seeds of the kiwi fruit add interesting texture and colour.

Serves 6
50g/2oz fresh root ginger
115g/4oz/generous ½ cup caster (superfine) sugar
300ml/½ pint/1¼ cups water
5 kiwi fruit
fresh mint sprigs or chopped kiwi fruit, to decorate

1 Peel the ginger and grate it finely. Put the sugar and water in a pan and heat gently until the sugar has dissolved. Add the ginger and cook for 1 minute, then leave to cool. Strain into a bowl and chill until very cold.

2 Peel the kiwi fruit, place in a blender and process to form a smooth purée. Add the purée to the chilled syrup and mix well.

3 Pour the kiwi mixture into a freezer container and freeze until slushy. Beat the mixture, then freeze again. Repeat this beating process one more time, then cover the container and freeze until firm.

4 Alternatively, use an ice cream maker. Freeze the mixture following the manufacturer's instructions, then transfer to a freezer container and freeze until required.

5 Remove the sorbet from the freezer 10–15 minutes before serving, to allow it to soften slightly. Spoon into glass bowls, then decorate with mint sprigs or pieces of chopped kiwi fruit and serve immediately.

Cook's Tip
Fresh ginger root is widely available and is easy to spot with its knobbly shape and pale brown skin. Look for smooth skin and firm solid flesh. Any left over can be wrapped and stored in the refrigerator for up to three weeks. Use a sharp knife for peeling.

Chocolate Sorbet Energy 179Kcal/758kJ; Protein 3.8g; Carbohydrate 31.2g, of which sugars 29.7g; Fat 5.3g, of which saturates 3.1g; Cholesterol 1mg; Calcium 44mg; Fibre 3.4g; Sodium 123mg.
Ginger & Kiwi Sorbet Energy 100Kcal/426kJ; Protein 0.7g; Carbohydrate 25.3g, of which sugars 25.2g; Fat 0.3g, of which saturates 0g; Cholesterol 0mg; Calcium 23mg; Fibre 1g; Sodium 3mg.

Chilli Sorbet

Served at a dinner party, as a palate tingling appetizer or a zingy dessert, this unusual sorbet is sure to become a talking point.

Serves 6
1 fresh medium-hot red chilli
finely grated rind and juice of
  2 lemons
finely grated rind and juice of
  2 limes
200g/7oz/1 cup caster (superfine)
  sugar
750ml/1¼ pints/3 cups water
lemon or lime rind, to decorate

1 Cut the chilli in half, removing all the seeds and any pith with a small sharp knife. Chop the flesh very finely.

2 Put the chilli, lemon and lime rind, sugar and water in a heavy pan. Heat gently and stir while the sugar dissolves. Bring to the boil, then simmer for 2 minutes without stirring. Leave to cool.

3 Add the lemon and lime juice to the chilli syrup and chill until very cold.

4 Pour the mixture into a freezer container and freeze for 3–4 hours, beating twice as it thickens. Return to the freezer until ready to serve.

5 Alternatively, use an ice cream maker. Freeze the mixture until it holds its shape. Scrape into a freezer container and freeze.

6 Soften slightly at room temperature before spooning into glasses and decorating with thinly pared lemon or lime rind.

> **Cook's Tips**
> • Wash your hands immediately after handling the chilli to avoid getting chilli juice in your eyes, should you rub them.
> • For an added kick to this sorbet, drizzle each portion with a little tequila or vodka before serving.

Lemon Sorbet

This is probably the most classic sorbet of all. Cooling and deliciously smooth, it literally melts in the mouth.

Serves 6
200g/7oz/1 cup caster
  (superfine) sugar
300ml/½ pint/1¼ cups water
4 lemons, well scrubbed
1 egg white

1 Put the sugar and water in a pan and bring to the boil, stirring occasionally until the sugar has just dissolved.

2 Using a swivel vegetable peeler, pare the rind thinly from two of the lemons so that it falls straight into the pan. Simmer for 2 minutes without stirring, then take the pan off the heat. Leave to cool, then chill.

3 Squeeze the juice from all the lemons and add to the syrup.

4 Strain the syrup into a shallow freezer container, reserving the rind. Freeze the mixture for 4 hours until it is mushy.

5 Scoop the sorbet into a food processor and process until smooth. Lightly whisk the egg white with a fork until it is just frothy. Spoon the sorbet back into the container, beat in the egg white and return the mixture to the freezer for 4 hours.

6 Alternatively, use an ice cream maker. Strain the lemon syrup, reserving the rind, and churn until thick. Add the egg white to the mixture and churn for a further 10–15 minutes until firm enough to scoop.

7 Scoop into bowls. Decorate with strips of the reserved rind.

> **Cook's Tip**
> Cut one-third off the top of a lemon and reserve as a lid. Squeeze the juice out of the rest. Remove any membrane and use the shell as a ready-made container for the sorbet.

Chilli Sorbet Energy 150Kcal/640kJ; Protein 0.5g; Carbohydrate 39.4g, of which sugars 39.4g; Fat 0.1g, of which saturates 0g; Cholesterol 0mg; Calcium 23mg; Fibre 0g; Sodium 3mg.
Lemon Sorbet Energy 135Kcal/574kJ; Protein 0.7g; Carbohydrate 35.1g, of which sugars 35.1g; Fat 0g, of which saturates 0g; Cholesterol 0mg; Calcium 19mg; Fibre 0g; Sodium 13mg.

Spiced Sorbet Pears

Pears poached in wine make an elegant dessert at any time of the year. In this recipe the cooked pears are hollowed out and filled with a delicious sorbet.

Serves 6
550ml/18fl oz/2½ cups red wine
2 cinnamon sticks, halved
115g/4oz/generous ½ cup caster
(superfine) sugar
6 plump pears

1 Put the wine, cinnamon sticks and sugar in a heavy pan that is big enough for the pears. Heat gently to dissolve the sugar.

2 Peel the pears, leaving the stalks attached, and stand upright in the syrup, taking care not to pack them too tightly. Cover and simmer very gently for 10–20 minutes until just tender, turning so they colour evenly.

3 Lift out the pears with a slotted spoon and set aside to cool. Boil the cooking juice briefly until reduced to 350ml/12fl oz/ 1½ cups. Set aside and leave to cool.

4 Cut a deep 2.5cm/1in slice off the top of each pear and reserve. Use an apple corer to remove the cores. Using a teaspoon, scoop out the centre of each pear, leaving a thick shell. Put the scooped-out flesh in a food processor or blender. Put the hollowed pears and their lids in the freezer.

5 Strain the reduced cooking juice, then set 75ml/5 tbsp aside for serving and add the rest to the food processor. Blend until smooth. Pour the mixture into a freezer container and freeze for 3–4 hours, beating twice as it thickens. Alternatively, use an ice cream maker and churn until the mixture holds its shape.

6 Using a teaspoon, pack the sorbet into the frozen pears, piling it up high. Top with the lids and return to the freezer overnight.

7 Remove the pears from the freezer and leave them to stand for about 30 minutes before serving. The pears should have softened but the sorbet should remain icy. Spoon the reserved syrup around each pear to serve.

Chocolate Sorbet

A cooling treat for chocolate lovers. Serve with crisp little biscuits (cookies) as a light way to end a meal.

Serves 6
150g/5oz dark (bittersweet)
chocolate, chopped
115g/4oz plain (semisweet)
chocolate, grated
225g/8oz/1 cup caster
(superfine) sugar
475ml/16fl oz/2 cups
water
chocolate curls, to decorate

1 Put all of the chocolate in a food processor, fitted with a metal blade, and process for approximately 20–30 seconds, or until finely chopped.

2 Place the sugar and water in a pan over medium heat. Bring to the boil, stirring until all of the sugar has completely dissolved. Boil for about 2 minutes, then remove the pan from the heat.

3 While the machine is running, carefully add the hot sugar-and-water syrup to the chocolate in the food processor. Keep the food processor running for 1–2 minutes until the chocolate is completely melted and the mixture is smooth, scraping down the bowl once.

4 Strain the chocolate mixture into a large measuring jug (cup) or bowl. Leave to cool completely, then chill, making sure that you stir the mixture occasionally.

5 Pour the chilled mixture into a freezer container and freeze until it is slushy.

6 Whisk until smooth, then freeze again until almost firm. Whisk for a second time and return to the freezer.

7 Allow to soften slightly before serving decorated with the chocolate curls.

Spiced Sorbet Pears Energy 198Kcal/835kJ; Protein 0.6g; Carbohydrate 35.2g, of which sugars 35.2g; Fat 0.2g, of which saturates 0g; Cholesterol 0mg; Calcium 33mg; Fibre 3.3g; Sodium 12mg.
Chocolate Sorbet Energy 301Kcal/1266kJ; Protein 2.3g; Carbohydrate 48.1g, of which sugars 47.7g; Fat 12.4g, of which saturates 7.4g; Cholesterol 3mg; Calcium 25mg; Fibre 1.1g; Sodium 4mg.

Raspberry Sorbet

This delicious sorbet is gloriously flavoured with both puréed and crushed fresh raspberries.

Serves 4

175g/6oz/¾ cup caster (superfine) sugar
150ml/¼ pint/⅔ cup water
500g/1¼lb/3½ cups raspberries, plus extra, to serve
500ml/17fl oz/generous 2 cups virtually fat-free fromage frais or low-fat cream cheese

1 Put the caster sugar and water in a small pan and bring to the boil, stirring until the sugar has dissolved. Pour into a jug (pitcher) and leave to cool.

2 Put 350g/12oz/2½ cups of the raspberries in a food processor or blender. Process to a purée, then press through a sieve (strainer) placed over a large bowl to remove the seeds. Stir the sugar syrup into the raspberry purée and chill the mixture until it is very cold.

3 Add the fromage frais to the purée and whisk until smooth.

4 Pour the mixture into a freezer container and freeze for 4 hours, beating twice as it freezes with a fork, electric whisk or in a food processor to break up the ice crystals.

5 Alternatively, use an ice cream maker, following the manufacturer's instructions. Churn the mixture until it is thick but too soft to scoop, then scrape into a freezer container. (If this quantity is too large for your machine, make it in two batches.)

6 Crush the remaining raspberries between your fingers and add them to the partially frozen ice cream. Mix lightly then freeze for 2–3 hours until firm.

7 Scoop the ice cream into individual dishes and serve with extra raspberries on top.

Ice Cream with Sweet Pine Nut Sauce

The delicious combination of lightly toasted pine nuts, tangy lemon and butter makes an easy sauce, perfect for enlivening vanilla ice cream and lemon sorbet.

Serves 4

75g/3oz/5 tbsp pine nuts
25g/1oz/2tbsp unsalted (sweet) butter
30ml/2 tbsp clear honey
30ml/2 tbsp light muscovado (brown) sugar
finely grated rind and juice of 1 lemon
250ml/8fl oz/1 cup lemon sorbet
250ml/8fl oz/1 cup vanilla ice cream

1 Toast the nuts lightly, shaking them until evenly coloured, then chop roughly. Melt the butter in a small, heavy pan with the honey and sugar. Remove from the heat. Stir in the lemon rind and juice.

2 Stir in the chopped pine nuts. Pour the sauce into a small jug (pitcher). Leave to cool until ready to serve.

3 To serve, alternate small scoops of the lemon sorbet and the vanilla ice cream in four tall serving glasses. Generously spoon the pine nut sauce over the ices and serve immediately.

Cook's Tips
• The sauce will be very thin while it is still warm, but it becomes thicker as it cools. It is best to serve the sauce before it has turned cold.
• Pine nuts, which are the seeds of a Mediterranean pine tree, have a softish, oily texture and an attractive, delicate flavour. You can toast the pine nuts in a variety of ways. Spread them on a baking sheet and toast in the oven or under the grill (broiler) for about 5 minutes, shaking them frequently. Alternatively, put the pine nuts in a dry non-stick frying pan and lightly toast over a medium heat, shaking often. Keep a close eye on them as they can over-brown very quickly.

Raspberry Sorbet Energy 276Kcal/1181kJ; Protein 11.6g; Carbohydrate 60g, of which sugars 60g; Fat 0.6g, of which saturates 0.3g; Cholesterol 1mg; Calcium 163mg; Fibre 3.1g; Sodium 48mg.
Ice Cream Energy 419Kcal/1756kJ; Protein 5.6g; Carbohydrate 48.1g, of which sugars 47.4g; Fat 23.4g, of which saturates 7.9g; Cholesterol 29mg; Calcium 71mg; Fibre 0.4g; Sodium 88mg.

Honeyed Goat's Milk Gelato

Goat's milk is much more widely available than it used to be and is more easily tolerated by some individuals than cow's milk. With this recipe, the milk is used to make a surprisingly rich iced dessert.

Serves 4
6 egg yolks
50g/2oz/¼ cup caster (superfine) sugar
10ml/2 tsp cornflour (cornstarch)
600ml/1 pint/2½ cups goat's milk
60ml/4 tbsp clear honey
pomegranate seeds, to decorate

1 Whisk the egg yolks, sugar and cornflour in a bowl until the mixture is pale and thick. Pour the goat's milk into a heavy pan, bring it to the boil, and then gradually whisk it into the egg yolk mixture.

2 Return the custard mixture to the pan and cook over a gentle heat, stirring constantly, until the custard thickens and is smooth. Pour it back into a clean bowl and stir in the honey. Leave to cool, then chill.

3 Pour the mixture into a freezer container and freeze for 6 hours until just firm enough to scoop, beating twice with a fork or in a food processor to break up the ice crystals.

4 To serve, scoop the ice cream into dishes and decorate with a few pomegranate seeds.

Variation/Banana Gelato

Make a syrup by heating 150ml/¼ pint/⅔ cup water and 115g/4oz/½ cup caster (superfine) sugar in a pan until the sugar dissolves completely. When the sugar syrup has cooled, add 3 mashed bananas and the juice of 1 lemon, plus 300ml/½ pint/1¼ cups vanilla-flavour soya dessert. Freeze for 6–7 hours until firm, beating twice within that time to break up any ice crystals.

Date & Tofu Ice

All you sceptics who claim to hate tofu, prepare to be converted by this creamy date and apple ice cream. Generously spiced with cinnamon, it not only tastes good but is packed with soya protein, contains no added sugar, is low in fat and free from all dairy products.

Serves 4
250g/9oz/1½ cups stoned (pitted) dates
600ml/1 pint/2½ cups apple juice
5ml/1 tsp ground cinnamon
285g/10½oz pack chilled tofu, drained and cubed
150ml/¼ pint/⅔ cup unsweetened soya milk

1 Put the dates in a pan. Pour in 300ml/½ pint/1¼ cups of the apple juice and leave to soak for 2 hours. Simmer for 10 minutes, then leave to cool. Using a slotted spoon, lift out one-quarter of the dates, chop roughly and set aside.

2 Purée the remaining dates in a food processor or blender. Add the cinnamon and process with enough of the remaining apple juice to make a smooth paste.

3 Add the cubes of tofu, a few at a time, processing after each addition. Finally, add the remaining apple juice and the soya milk.

4 Pour the mixture into a freezer container and freeze for 4 hours, beating twice to break up the ice crystals.

5 Alternatively, use an ice cream maker. Churn until thick, but not firm enough to scoop. Turn into a freezer container.

6 Stir in most of the chopped dates and freeze for 2–3 hours until firm. To serve, scoop the ice into dessert glasses and decorate with the remaining chopped dates.

Cook's Tip
As tofu is a non-dairy product, it will not blend completely, so don't be concerned if the mixture contains tiny flecks of tofu.

Goat's Milk Gelato Energy 255Kcal/1075kJ; Protein 7.7g; Carbohydrate 33.4g, of which sugars 31.1g; Fat 11.1g, of which saturates 5.1g; Cholesterol 218mg; Calcium 181mg; Fibre 0g; Sodium 76mg.
Date & Tofu Ice Energy 290Kcal/1232kJ; Protein 9.1g; Carbohydrate 58.2g, of which sugars 57.9g; Fat 3.9g, of which saturates 0.5g; Cholesterol 0mg; Calcium 407mg; Fibre 2.5g; Sodium 24mg.

Coconut Ice

Despite its creamy taste, this ice cream contains neither cream nor egg and is very refreshing. Serve it with scoops of fresh summer fruits.

Serves 4–6
150ml/¼ pint/⅔ cup water
115g/4oz/generous ½ cup caster (superfine) sugar
2 limes
400ml/14fl oz can coconut milk
toasted coconut shavings, to decorate

1 Put the water in a small pan. Add the caster sugar and bring to the boil, stirring constantly until the sugar has completely dissolved. Remove the pan from the heat and leave the syrup to cool, then chill well.

2 Grate the limes finely, taking care to avoid the bitter pith. Squeeze the fruit and pour the juice and rind into the pan of syrup. Add the coconut milk.

3 Pour the mixture into a freezer container and freeze for 5–6 hours until firm, beating twice with a fork, electric whisk or in a food processor to break up the ice crystals.

4 Alternatively, use an ice cream maker and churn the mixture until firm enough to scoop, then transfer to a freezer container and freeze until required.

5 To serve, scoop the coconut ice into individual dishes and decorate with toasted coconut shavings.

Cook's Tip
To make toasted coconut shavings, you will need a peeled piece of fresh coconut. First, rinse the fresh coconut with cold water, then cut off thin slices using a vegetable peeler. Toast the slices under a moderate grill (broiler) until the coconut has curled and the edges have turned golden. Cool slightly, then use as a pretty decoration for the coconut ice.

Mascarpone & Raspberry Ripple

Mascarpone makes a wonderfully smooth base for ice cream, which is made even more delicious when mixed with a tangy lemon syrup and streaked with raspberry purée.

Serves 8
250g/9oz/1¼ cups caster (superfine) sugar
450ml/¾ pint/scant 2 cups water
finely grated rind and juice of 1 lemon
350g/12oz/2 cups raspberries, plus extra to decorate
500g/1¼lb/2½ cups mascarpone

1 Put 225g/8oz/1 cup of the sugar in a heavy pan. Pour in the water and heat gently until the sugar dissolves. Bring to the boil, add the lemon rind and juice and boil for 3 minutes, without stirring, to make a syrup. Leave to cool.

2 Crush the raspberries lightly with a fork until broken up but not completely puréed, then stir in the remaining sugar.

3 Beat the mascarpone in a large bowl until smooth, gradually adding the lemon syrup.

4 Pour the mascarpone mixture into a freezer container and freeze until it begins to thicken. Beat to break down the ice crystals, then return to the freezer. When beginning to thicken again, repeat the beating process for a second time, then return to the freezer until the ice cream is frozen but still soft.

5 Alternatively, use an ice cream maker. Churn the mixture until thick, then transfer to a freezer container.

6 Spoon the crushed raspberries over the ice cream. Using a metal spoon, fold into the ice cream until rippled, making sure you reach the corners. Freeze for several hours or overnight until firm.

7 To serve, scoop the ice cream into glasses and decorate with the extra raspberries.

Chocolate Flake Ice Cream

This enticing ice cream, speckled with chocolate, is difficult to resist. Serve with slices of tropical fruit, such as pineapple and mango, for a perfect balance.

Serves 6
300ml/½ pint/1¼ cups whipping
   cream, chilled
90ml/6 tbsp Greek (US strained
   plain) yogurt
75–90ml/5–6 tbsp caster
   (superfine) sugar
few drops of vanilla extract
150g/5oz/10 tbsp flaked or
   roughly grated chocolate
flaked chocolate pieces, to
   decorate

1 Have ready a 600–900ml/1–1½ pint/2½–3¾ cup freezer container, preferably with a lid.

2 Softly whip the cream in a large bowl then fold in the yogurt, sugar, vanilla extract and chocolate. Stir gently to mix thoroughly, and then transfer to the freezer container.

3 Smooth the surface of the ice cream, then cover and freeze. Gently stir with a fork every 30 minutes for up to 4 hours until the ice cream is too hard to stir.

4 Alternatively, use an ice cream maker. Freeze the cream and chocolate mixture following the manufacturer's instructions.

5 Transfer to the refrigerator 15 minutes before serving to soften slightly. Serve in scoops, decorated with chocolate flakes.

> **Cook's Tips**
> • *Transferring the ice cream to the refrigerator for a short time before serving allows the full flavour of the dessert to develop and makes it easier to scoop it into neat balls.*
> • *Use a metal scoop to serve the ice cream, dipping the scoop briefly in warm water between servings.*

Chocolate Ice Cream

To make this popular classic, use good quality chocolate to give the best flavour.

Serves 6
750ml/1¼ pints/3 cups milk
10cm/4in piece of vanilla pod
   (bean)
4 egg yolks
150g/5oz/¾ cup granulated
   sugar
225g/8oz dark (bittersweet)
   chocolate, melted

1 To make the custard, heat the milk with the vanilla pod in a small pan. Remove from the heat as soon as small bubbles start to form. Do not boil.

2 Beat the egg yolks with a wire whisk or electric beater. Gradually incorporate the sugar, and continue beating for about 5 minutes until the mixture is pale yellow. Strain the milk and slowly add it to the egg mixture, drop by drop.

3 Pour the mixture into a double boiler with the melted chocolate. Stir over moderate heat until the water in the pan is boiling, and the custard thickens enough to lightly coat the back of a spoon. Remove from the heat and allow to cool.

4 Pour the mixture into a freezer container and freeze until set, about 3 hours. Remove from the container and chop roughly into 7.5cm/3in pieces. Place in the bowl of a food processor and process until smooth. Return to the freezer container, and freeze again until firm. Repeat the freezing-chopping process 2 or 3 times, until a smooth consistency is reached, then freeze until required. Alternatively, use an ice cream maker and freeze the mixture following the manufacturer's instructions.

> **Cook's Tip**
> *If you do not have a double boiler, cook the custard in a heatproof bowl set over a pan of water. Make sure that the custard does not boil, otherwise it will curdle.*

Choc. Ice Cream Energy 388Kcal/1634kJ; Protein 8.2g; Carbohydrate 55.8g, of which sugars 55.5g; Fat 16.3g, of which saturates 8.7g; Cholesterol 144mg; Calcium 191mg; Fibre 0.9g; Sodium 64mg.
Choc. Flake Ice Energy 385Kcal/1600kJ; Protein 3.3g; Carbohydrate 30.6g, of which sugars 30.4g; Fat 28.7g, of which saturates 17.6g; Cholesterol 54mg; Calcium 66mg; Fibre 0.6g; Sodium 25mg.

White Chocolate Raspberry Ripple

A truly luscious treat that always impresses. Note that an ice cream maker is required for this recipe.

Serves 6
250ml/8fl oz/1 cup milk
475ml/16fl oz/2 cups whipping cream
7 egg yolks
30ml/2 tbsp granulated sugar
225g/8oz good white chocolate, chopped into small pieces
5ml/1 tsp vanilla extract
mint sprigs, to decorate

For the sauce
275g/10oz raspberry preserve or 275g/10oz frozen raspberries in light syrup
10ml/2 tsp golden (light corn) syrup
15ml/1 tbsp lemon juice
15ml/1 tbsp cornflour (cornstarch), if using frozen fruit in syrup, mixed with 15ml/1 tbsp water

1 For the sauce, put the preserve in a pan with the golden syrup, the lemon juice and the water but not the cornflour. If using frozen fruit, press the fruit and its syrup through a sieve (strainer) into a pan and add all the other sauce ingredients. Bring to the boil, stirring. Simmer for 1–2 minutes. Pour into a bowl, cool, then chill.

2 In a pan, combine the milk and 250ml/8fl oz/1 cup of the cream and bring to the boil. In a bowl, beat the yolks and sugar with a hand-held mixer for 2–3 minutes until thick and creamy. Gradually pour the hot milk mixture over the yolks and return to the pan. Cook over a medium heat, stirring constantly, until the custard coats the back of a wooden spoon.

3 Remove the pan from the heat and stir in the white chocolate until melted and smooth. Pour the remaining cream into a large bowl. Strain in the hot custard, mix well, then stir in the vanilla extract. Cool, then freeze in an ice cream maker.

4 When frozen but soft, transfer one-third of the ice cream to a freezerproof bowl. Set aside half the raspberry sauce, spooning a third of the rest over the ice cream. Cover with another third of the ice cream and more sauce. Repeat. With a knife, lightly marble the mixture. Cover and freeze. Let the ice cream soften for 15 minutes. Serve with the rest of the raspberry sauce, and the mint.

Chocolate Ripple Ice Cream

This creamy, dark chocolate ice cream, unevenly rippled with swirls of rich chocolate sauce, will stay deliciously soft even after freezing.

Serves 4–6
4 egg yolks
75g/3oz/6 tbsp caster (superfine) sugar
5ml/1 tsp cornflour (cornstarch)
300ml/½ pint/1¼ cups semi-skimmed (low-fat) milk
250g/9oz dark (bittersweet) chocolate, broken into squares
25g/1oz/2 tbsp butter, diced
30ml/2 tbsp golden (light corn) syrup
90ml/6 tbsp single (light) cream or cream and milk mixed
300ml/½ pint/1¼ cups whipping cream

1 Put the egg yolks, sugar and cornflour in a bowl and whisk until thick and foamy. Pour the milk into a heavy pan, bring just to the boil, then gradually pour the milk on to the yolk mixture, whisking constantly.

2 Return the mixture to the pan and cook over a gentle heat, stirring constantly until the custard thickens and is smooth. Pour back into the bowl and stir in 150g/5oz of the chocolate until melted. Cover the custard closely, leave to cool, then chill.

3 Put the remaining chocolate in a pan with the butter and golden syrup. Heat gently, stirring, until melted. Stir in the single cream or cream and milk mixture. Heat gently, stirring, until smooth then leave to cool.

4 Whip the cream until it has thickened, but is still soft enough to fall from a spoon. Fold it into the custard, pour into a freezer container and freeze for 5 hours until thick, beating twice with a fork or in a food processor during this time.

5 Alternatively, use an ice cream maker. Stir the whipped cream into the cooled custard and churn the mixture for 20–25 minutes until thick.

6 Add alternate spoonfuls of ice cream and sauce to a large freezer container. Freeze for 5–6 hours until firm.

White Chocolate Energy 735Kcal/3066kJ; Protein 10.3g; Carbohydrate 63.3g, of which sugars 61g; Fat 50.8g, of which saturates 29.2g; Cholesterol 321mg; Calcium 242mg; Fibre 1.2g; Sodium 110mg.
Chocolate Energy 594Kcal/2474kJ; Protein 7.3g; Carbohydrate 48.3g, of which sugars 47.2g; Fat 42.6g, of which saturates 25.2g; Cholesterol 209mg; Calcium 140mg; Fibre 1.1g; Sodium 87mg.

Chocolate Ice Cream with Lime Sabayon

Sabayon sauce has a light, foamy texture that perfectly complements the rich, smooth flavour of ice cream. This tangy lime version is particularly delicious when spooned generously over chocolate ice cream.

Serves 4

2 egg yolks
65g/2½oz/5 tbsp caster (superfine) sugar
finely grated rind and juice of 2 limes
60ml/4 tbsp white wine or apple juice
45ml/3 tbsp single (light) cream
500ml/17fl oz/2¼ cups chocolate chip or dark (bittersweet) chocolate ice cream
pared strips of lime rind, to decorate

1 Put the egg yolks and sugar in a heatproof bowl and beat until combined. Beat in the lime rind and juice, then the white wine or apple juice.

2 Whisk the mixture over a pan of gently simmering water until the sabayon is smooth and thick, and the mixture leaves a trail when the whisk is lifted from the bowl. Lightly whisk in the cream. Remove the bowl from the pan and cover with a lid or plate.

3 Working quickly, scoop the ice cream into four glasses. Spoon the sabayon sauce over the ice cream, decorate with the strips of lime rind and serve immediately.

Variation

The tangy lime sauce marries just as well with vanilla ice cream. It is also very good served with individual servings of sliced tropical fruit – pineapple, papaya and kiwi would look pretty. Try the sabayon sauce as a topping for a selection of soft summer fruits, too.

Rocky Road Ice Cream

A gloriously rich ice cream with lots of texture.

Serves 6

115g/4oz plain (semisweet) chocolate, chopped into small pieces
150ml/¼ pint/⅔ cup milk
300ml/½ pint/1¼ cups double (heavy) cream
115g/4oz/2 cups marshmallows, chopped
115g/4oz/½ cup glacé (candied) cherries, chopped
50g/2oz/½ cup crumbled shortbread
30ml/2 tbsp chopped walnuts
chocolate sauce and wafers, to serve (optional)

1 Melt the chocolate in the milk in a pan over a gentle heat, stirring from time to time. Pour into a bowl and leave to cool.

2 Whip the cream in a separate bowl until it just holds its shape. Beat in the chocolate mixture, a little at a time, until the mixture is smooth and creamy.

3 Pour the chocolate mixture into a freezer container and transfer to the freezer. Freeze until ice crystals form around the edges, then whisk with a strong hand whisk or hand-held electric mixer until smooth. Alternatively, use an ice cream maker and churn the mixture until almost frozen, following the manufacturer's instructions.

4 Stir the marshmallows, glacé cherries, crumbled shortbread and nuts into the iced mixture, then return to the freezer container and freeze until firm.

5 Allow the ice cream to soften at room temperature for 15–20 minutes before serving in scoops. Add a wafer and chocolate sauce to each portion, if you wish.

Cook's Tip

Do not allow the mixture to freeze too hard before step 4, otherwise it will be difficult to stir in the remaining ingredients.

Chocolate Energy 395Kcal/1648kJ; Protein 6.8g; Carbohydrate 38.3g, of which sugars 38.2g; Fat 23.8g, of which saturates 13.5g; Cholesterol 107mg; Calcium 157mg; Fibre 0g; Sodium 84mg.
Rocky Road Energy 545Kcal/2271kJ; Protein 4.7g; Carbohydrate 48.3g, of which sugars 40.6g; Fat 38.4g, of which saturates 22g; Cholesterol 77mg; Calcium 85mg; Fibre 1g; Sodium 57mg.

Crème Fraîche & Honey Ice

This delicately flavoured ice cream is lovely served on its own, but is also good with a fruit pie or crumble.

Serves 4

4 egg yolks
60ml/4 tbsp clear flower honey
5ml/1 tsp cornflour (cornstarch)

300ml/½ pint/1¼ cups
    semi-skimmed (low-fat) milk
7.5ml/1½ tsp vanilla
    extract
250g/9oz/generous 1 cup
    crème fraîche
nasturtium, pansy or herb flowers,
    to decorate

1 Whisk the egg yolks, honey and cornflour in a bowl until thick and foamy. Pour the milk into a heavy pan, bring to the boil, then gradually pour on to the yolk mixture in the bowl, whisking constantly.

2 Return the mixture to the pan and cook over a gentle heat, stirring all the time until the custard thickens and is smooth. Pour it back into the bowl, then chill.

3 Stir in the vanilla extract and crème fraîche. Pour into a freezer container. Freeze for 6 hours or until firm enough to scoop, beating once or twice with a fork or in a food processor to break up the ice crystals.

4 Alternatively, use an ice cream maker. Stir the vanilla extract and crème fraîche into the chilled honey custard mixture and churn until thick and firm enough to scoop, following the manufacturer's instructions.

5 Serve in glass dishes and decorate with nasturtiums, pansies or herb flowers.

> **Cook's Tip**
> *Measure the honey carefully and use level spoonfuls; if you are over-generous, the honey flavour will dominate and the ice cream will be too sweet.*

Classic Vanilla Ice Cream

Nothing beats the creamy simplicity of true vanilla ice cream. Vanilla pods are expensive, but well worth buying for the superb flavour they impart.

Serves 4

1 vanilla pod (bean)
300ml/½ pint/1¼ cups
    semi-skimmed (low-fat) milk
4 egg yolks
75g/3oz/6 tbsp caster (superfine)
    sugar
5ml/1 tsp cornflour (cornstarch)
300ml/½ pint/1¼ cups
    double (heavy) cream

1 Using a small knife, slit the vanilla pod lengthways. Pour the milk into a heavy pan, add the vanilla pod and bring to the boil. Remove from the heat and leave for 15 minutes to allow the flavours to infuse.

2 Lift the vanilla pod up. Holding it over the pan, scrape the black seeds out of the pod with a small knife so that they fall back into the milk. Set the vanilla pod aside and bring the milk back to the boil.

3 Whisk the egg yolks, sugar and cornflour in a bowl until the mixture is thick and foamy. Gradually pour on the hot milk, whisking constantly. Return the mixture to the pan and cook over a gentle heat, stirring constantly.

4 When the custard is thick and smooth, pour it back into the bowl. Leave to cool, then chill.

5 Whip the cream until it has thickened but still falls from a spoon. Fold it into the custard and pour into a freezer container. Freeze for 6 hours or until firm enough to scoop, beating twice with a fork or in a food processor.

6 Alternatively, use an ice cream maker. Stir the cream into the custard and churn the mixture until thick.

7 Serve scooped into dishes, bowls or bought cones.

Crème Fraîche Ice Energy 386Kcal/1602kJ; Protein 6.9g; Carbohydrate 16.5g, of which sugars 16.3g; Fat 33g, of which saturates 19.5g; Cholesterol 277mg; Calcium 151mg; Fibre 0g; Sodium 57mg.
Classic Vanilla Energy 546Kcal/2264kJ; Protein 6.8g; Carbohydrate 25.6g, of which sugars 24.4g; Fat 47.1g, of which saturates 27.4g; Cholesterol 309mg; Calcium 160mg; Fibre 0g; Sodium 60mg.

Coconut & Lemon Grass Ice Cream

The combination of cream and coconut milk makes for a wonderfully rich ice cream. The lemon grass flavouring adds a subtle tang to the dish.

Serves 4
2 lemon grass stalks
475ml/16fl oz/2 cups double (heavy) cream
120ml/4fl oz/½ cup coconut milk
4 large (US extra large) eggs
105ml/7 tbsp caster (superfine) sugar
5ml/1 tsp vanilla extract

1 Cut the lemon grass stalks in half lengthways. Use a mallet or rolling pin to mash the pieces, breaking up the fibres so that all the flavour is released.

2 Pour the cream and coconut milk into a pan. Add the lemon grass stalks and heat gently, stirring frequently, until the mixture starts to simmer.

3 Put the eggs, sugar and vanilla extract in a large bowl. Using an electric whisk, whisk until the mixture is very light and fluffy.

4 Strain the cream mixture into a heatproof bowl that will fit over a pan of simmering water. Whisk in the egg mixture, then place the bowl over the pan and continue to whisk until the mixture thickens. Remove from the heat and leave to cool. Chill the coconut custard in the refrigerator for 3–4 hours.

5 Pour the mixture into a freezer container. Freeze for 4 hours, beating two or three times at hourly intervals with a fork to break up the ice crystals.

6 Alternatively, use an ice cream maker. Pour the chilled mixture into the machine and churn until it is firm enough to scoop. Serve immediately, or scrape into a freezer container and transfer to the freezer.

7 About 30 minutes before serving, transfer the container to the refrigerator so that the ice cream softens slightly. Serve in scoops.

Orange Flower Water Ice Cream

Delicately perfumed with orange flower water, this nutty ice cream is filled with flavours popular in the Middle East.

Serves 4–6
4 egg yolks
75g/3oz/6 tbsp caster (superfine) sugar
5ml/1 tsp cornflour (cornstarch)
300ml/½ pint/1¼ cups semi-skimmed (low-fat) milk
300ml/½ pint/1¼ cups whipping cream
150g/5oz/1¼ cups cashew nuts, finely chopped
15ml/1 tbsp orange flower water
grated rind of ½ orange, plus spirals of orange rind, to decorate

1 Whisk the egg yolks, sugar and cornflour in a bowl until thick. Pour the milk into a pan and bring it to the boil. Whisk it into the egg yolk mixture.

2 Return to the pan and cook over a low heat, stirring constantly, until very smooth. Pour back into the bowl. Leave to cool, then chill.

3 Heat the cream in a pan. When it has come to the boil, stir in the chopped cashew nuts. Leave to cool.

4 Stir the orange flower water and grated orange rind into the chilled custard. Process the cashew nut cream in a food processor or blender until it forms a fine paste, then stir it into the custard mixture.

5 Pour the mixture into a freezer container and freeze for 6 hours, beating twice with a fork or whisking briefly with an electric mixer, to break up the ice crystals and obtain a smooth consistency.

6 Alternatively, use an ice cream maker and churn the mixture until it is firm enough to scoop.

7 To serve, scoop the ice cream into dishes and decorate with orange rind curls.

Lemon Grass Energy 773Kcal/3200kJ; Protein 8.4g; Carbohydrate 30.9g, of which sugars 30.9g; Fat 69.4g, of which saturates 41.3g; Cholesterol 353mg; Calcium 109mg; Fibre 0g; Sodium 131mg.
Water Ice Energy 410Kcal/1696kJ; Protein 9.8g; Carbohydrate 9.2g, of which sugars 5.1g; Fat 37.4g, of which saturates 16.7g; Cholesterol 190mg; Calcium 114mg; Fibre 0.8g; Sodium 113mg.

Brandied Fruit & Rice Ice Cream

This combines spicy rice pudding with a creamy egg custard.

Serves 4–6

50g/2oz/¼ cup ready-to-eat pitted prunes, chopped
50g/2oz/¼ cup ready-to-eat dried apricots, chopped
50g/2oz/¼ cup glacé (candied) cherries, chopped
30ml/2 tbsp brandy
150ml/¼ pint/⅔ cup single (light) cream

For the rice mixture

40g/1½oz/generous ¼ cup pudding (short grain) rice
450ml/¾ pint/scant 2 cups milk
1 cinnamon stick, halved, plus extra to decorate
4 cloves

For the custard

4 egg yolks
75g/3oz/6 tbsp caster (superfine) sugar
5ml/1 tsp cornflour (cornstarch)
300ml/½ pint/1¼ cups milk

1 Put the chopped dried fruit in a bowl. Pour over the brandy. Cover and leave to soak for 3 hours or overnight, if possible.

2 Put the rice, milk and spices in a pan. Bring to the boil, then simmer gently for 30 minutes, stirring occasionally until most of the milk has been absorbed. Lift out the spices. Let the rice cool.

3 Whisk the egg yolks, sugar and cornflour in a bowl until thick and foamy. Heat the milk in a heavy pan, then gradually pour it on to the yolks, whisking constantly. Pour back into the pan and cook, stirring until the custard thickens. Leave to cool, then chill.

4 Mix the chilled custard, rice and cream together. Pour into a freezer container and freeze for 4–5 hours until mushy, then beat lightly with a fork to break up the ice crystals.

5 Fold in the fruits then freeze for 2–3 hours until firm enough to scoop. Alternatively, use an ice cream maker. Mix the chilled custard, rice and cream together and churn until thick. Spoon the ice cream into a freezer container and fold in the fruits. Freeze for 2–3 hours until firm.

6 Serve scoops of ice cream decorated with cinnamon sticks.

Coffee Ice Cream

This classic ice cream is always a favourite and, despite its simplicity, has an air of sophistication and elegance about it.

Serves 8

600ml/1 pint/2½ cups fresh ready-made custard
150ml/¼ pint/⅔ cup strong black coffee
300ml/½ pint/1¼ cups double (heavy) cream

1 Put the custard in a large bowl and stir in the coffee. In a separate bowl, whip the cream until it has a soft texture but is not stiff, and then fold the whipped cream evenly into the coffee and custard mixture.

2 Pour the mixture into a freezer container and cover with a tight-fitting lid or clear film (plastic wrap) and place in the freezer for about 2 hours until beginning to freeze.

3 Remove the ice cream from the freezer and beat with a fork to break up the ice crystals.

4 Return the ice cream to the freezer, freeze for a further 2 hours, then beat again with a fork. Return to the freezer until completely frozen.

5 Alternatively, use an ice cream maker. Pour the coffee and custard mixture into the machine and churn until firm.

6 Serve scooped into individual dishes.

Cook's Tips

• For a good flavour, it is best to make the coffee from ground coffee beans brewed in a cafetière, for instance, or made by the filter method. Coffee made from instant granules is perfectly adequate as long you make it quite strong.
• Coffee beans make a complementary decoration for individual portions of ice cream.

Brandied Fruit & Rice Energy 293Kcal/1228kJ; Protein 8g; Carbohydrate 36.7g, of which sugars 30.7g; Fat 13.4g, of which saturates 7.2g; Cholesterol 166mg; Calcium 207mg; Fibre 1.1g; Sodium 73mg.
Coffee Ice Cream Energy 260Kcal/1076kJ; Protein 2.6g; Carbohydrate 12.9g, of which sugars 10.2g; Fat 21.5g, of which saturates 12.5g; Cholesterol 53mg; Calcium 87mg; Fibre 0.1g; Sodium 39mg.

Pecan-Topped Coffee Ice Cream

Heavenly ice cream, topped with sweetened nuts.

Serves 4–6
300ml/½ pint/1¼ cups milk
1 tbsp demerara (raw) sugar
25g/1oz/3 tbsp finely ground
    coffee or 15ml/1 tbsp instant
    coffee granules

1 egg plus 2 yolks
300ml/½ pint/1¼ cups double
    (heavy) cream
15ml/1 tbsp caster (superfine) sugar

For the pecans
115g/4oz/1 cup pecan halves
50g/2oz/¼ cup soft dark
    brown sugar

1 Heat the milk and demerara sugar to boiling point. Remove from the heat and sprinkle on the coffee. Leave to stand for 2 minutes, then stir, cover and cool.

2 In a heatproof bowl, beat the egg and extra yolks until the mixture is thick and pale.

3 Strain the coffee mixture into a clean pan, heat to boiling point, then pour on to the eggs in a steady stream, beating constantly. Set the bowl over a pan of gently simmering water and stir until it thickens. Cool, then chill in the refrigerator.

4 Whip the cream with the caster sugar. Fold it into the coffee custard and freeze in a covered container. Beat twice at hourly intervals, then leave to freeze firm.

5 To caramelize the nuts, preheat the oven to 180°C/350°F/ Gas 4. Spread the nuts on a baking sheet in a layer. Toast them in the oven for 10–15 minutes until they release their fragrance.

6 Dissolve the brown sugar in 30ml/2 tbsp water in a heavy pan, shaking over a low heat until it dissolves. When the syrup begins to bubble, add the pecans and cook for 1–2 minutes over medium heat until the syrup coats the nuts.

7 Spread the nuts on a lightly oiled baking sheet, separating them with the tip of a knife. Leave to cool. Soften the ice cream in the refrigerator for 30 minutes, then serve with the nuts.

Chocolate Mint Ice Cream Pie

This chocolate-flavoured cereal pie case is incredibly easy to make and offers a simple way to turn ready-made ice cream into a smart-looking dessert.

Serves 8
75g/3oz plain (semisweet)
    chocolate chips
40g/1½oz/3 tbsp butter or
    margarine
50g/2oz crisped rice cereal
1 litre/1¾ pints/4 cups mint-
    chocolate-chip ice cream
chocolate curls, to decorate

1 Line a 23cm/9in pie tin (pan) with foil. Place a round of baking parchment over the foil in the bottom of the tin.

2 Put the chocolate chips and butter or margarine in a heatproof bowl that will fit over a pan of simmering water. Place the bowl over the pan and melt the chocolate and butter.

3 Remove the bowl from the heat and gently stir in the cereal, a little at a time.

4 Press the chocolate-cereal mixture evenly over the base and up the sides of the prepared tin, forming a 1cm/½in rim. Chill until completely hard.

5 Carefully remove the cereal case from the tin and peel off the foil and paper. Return the case to the pie tin.

6 Remove the ice cream from the freezer. Let it soften for 10 minutes and spread it evenly in the cereal case. Freeze until firm.

7 Sprinkle the ice cream with chocolate curls just before serving.

Variation
Use any flavour of ice cream that marries well with chocolate – coffee, orange or raspberry ripple would be a good choice. Try plain, milk or white chocolate for the base.

White Chocolate Parfait

The ultimate cold dessert – white and dark chocolate in one mouthwatering slice.

Serves 10

225g/8oz white chocolate, chopped
600ml/1 pint/2½ cups whipping cream
120ml/4fl oz/½ cup milk
10 egg yolks
15ml/1 tbsp caster (superfine) sugar
25g/1oz/scant ½ cup desiccated (dry unsweetened shredded) coconut
120ml/4fl oz/½ cup canned sweetened coconut milk
150g/5oz/1¼ cups unsalted macadamia nuts

For the chocolate icing
225g/8oz plain (semisweet) chocolate
75g/3oz/6 tbsp butter
20ml/generous 1 tbsp golden (light corn) syrup
175ml/6fl oz/¾ cup whipping cream
curls of fresh coconut, to decorate

1 Line the base and sides of a 1.4 litre/2⅓ pint/6 cup terrine mould (25 × 10cm/10 × 4in) with clear film (plastic wrap).

2 Place the white chocolate and 120ml/4fl oz/½ cup of the cream in the top of a double boiler or in a heatproof bowl set over hot water. Stir until melted and smooth. Set aside.

3 Put 250ml/8fl oz/1 cup of the cream and the milk in a pan and bring to boiling point.

4 Meanwhile, whisk the egg yolks and caster sugar together in a large bowl, until thick and pale.

5 Add the hot cream mixture to the yolks, beating constantly. Pour back into the pan and cook over a low heat for 2–3 minutes, until thickened. Stir constantly and do not boil. Remove the pan from the heat. Add the melted chocolate, desiccated coconut and coconut milk, then stir well and leave to cool.

6 Whip the remaining cream until thick, then fold into the chocolate and coconut mixture.

7 Put 475ml/16fl oz/2 cups of the parfait mixture in the prepared mould and spread evenly. Cover and freeze for about 2 hours, until just firm. Cover the remaining mixture and chill.

8 Scatter the macadamia nuts evenly over the frozen parfait. Pour in the remaining parfait mixture. Cover the terrine and freeze for 6–8 hours or overnight, until the parfait is firm.

9 To make the icing, melt the chocolate with the butter and syrup in the top of a double boiler set over hot water. Stir occasionally. Heat the cream in a pan, until just simmering, then stir into the chocolate mixture. Remove from the heat; cool.

10 To turn out the parfait, wrap the terrine in a hot towel and invert on to a plate. Lift off the mould and clear film and place the parfait on a rack over a baking sheet. Pour the chocolate icing over the top and quickly smooth it down the sides with a palette knife. Leave to set slightly, then freeze for 3–4 hours. To serve, slice with a knife dipped in hot water and decorate with coconut curls.

Iced Praline Torte

This lovely torte will serve you well on any occasion.

Serves 8
115g/4oz/1 cup almonds
115g/4oz/generous ½ cup caster (superfine) sugar
115g/4oz/⅔ cup raisins
90ml/6 tbsp rum or brandy
115g/4oz dark (bittersweet) chocolate, broken into squares
30ml/2 tbsp milk
450ml/¾ pint/scant 2 cups double (heavy) cream
30ml/2 tbsp strong black coffee
16 sponge fingers

To finish
150ml/¼ pint/⅔ cup double (heavy) cream
50g/2oz/½ cup flaked (sliced) almonds, toasted
15g/½oz dark (bittersweet) chocolate, melted

1 To make the praline, oil a baking sheet. Put the nuts into a heavy pan with the sugar and heat gently until the sugar melts and coats the nuts. Cook slowly until the nuts brown and the sugar caramelizes. Transfer the nuts quickly to the sheet; leave until cold. Break up and grind to a fine powder in a blender.

2 Soak the raisins in 45ml/3 tbsp of the rum or brandy for at least an hour to soften and absorb the rum. Melt the chocolate with the milk in a bowl over a pan of hot, but not boiling water. Remove and leave until cold. Lightly grease a 1.2 litre/2 pint/ 5 cup loaf tin (pan) and line it with baking parchment.

3 Whisk the cream in a bowl until it holds soft peaks. Whisk in the chocolate. Fold in the praline and the raisins, with any liquid.

4 Mix the coffee and remaining rum or brandy in a shallow dish. Dip in the sponge fingers and arrange half in a layer over the base of the prepared loaf tin. Cover with the chocolate mixture and add another layer of soaked sponge fingers. Leave in the freezer overnight.

5 To finish, whip the double cream. Dip the tin briefly in warm water and turn the torte out on to a serving plate. Cover with the whipped cream, sprinkle the top with toasted almonds and drizzle with melted chocolate. Freeze until needed.

Parfait Energy 792Kcal/3280kJ; Protein 9.2g; Carbohydrate 34.8g, of which sugars 34.5g; Fat 69.4g, of which saturates 36g; Cholesterol 301mg; Calcium 165mg; Fibre 1.7g; Sodium 169mg.
Praline Torte Energy 636Kcal/2650kJ; Protein 7.7g; Carbohydrate 49.5g, of which sugars 43.5g; Fat 43.9g, of which saturates 22.3g; Cholesterol 134mg; Calcium 104mg; Fibre 1.9g; Sodium 47mg.

Pistachio & Nougat Torte

In this easy-to-prepare torte, nougat is combined with nuts, honey and rose water to create a fragrantly flavoured iced dessert.

Serves 8
75g/3oz/½ cup unsalted pistachio nuts, shelled
150g/5oz nougat
300ml/½ pint/1¼ cups whipping cream
90ml/6 tbsp clear honey
30ml/2 tbsp rose water
250g/9oz/generous 1 cup fromage frais or mascarpone
8 trifle sponges
icing (confectioners') sugar, for dusting
fresh raspberries, poached apricots or cherries, to serve (optional)

1 Soak the pistachio nuts in boiling water for 2 minutes. Drain them thoroughly, then rub them between pieces of kitchen paper to remove the skins. Peel off any skins that remain, then chop the nuts roughly.

2 Using a small sharp knife or scissors, cut the nougat into small pieces. Pour the cream into a bowl, add the honey and rose water and whip until it is just beginning to hold its shape.

3 Stir in the fromage frais or mascarpone, chopped pistachio nuts and nougat, and mix well. Slice the trifle sponges horizontally into three very thin layers.

4 Line a 15–17cm/6–6½in square loose-based cake tin (pan) with baking parchment or clear film (plastic wrap). Arrange a layer of sponges on the bottom, trimming the pieces to fit.

5 Pack the prepared filling into the cake tin and level the surface. Cover with the remaining sponges, then cover and freeze overnight.

6 Transfer the torte to the refrigerator about one hour before serving, then invert the torte on to a serving plate and dust with icing sugar. Serve with raspberries, poached apricots or cherries, if you like.

White Chocolate & Brownie Torte

An exceedingly rich dessert, this quick dish is guaranteed to appeal to chocolate lovers. The great thing about this recipe is that it uses very few ingredients, making shopping a breeze.

Serves 10
300g/11oz white chocolate, broken into pieces
600ml/1 pint/2½ cups double (heavy) cream
250g/9oz rich chocolate brownies
cocoa powder (unsweetened), for dusting

1 Dampen the sides of a 20cm/8in springform tin (pan) and line with a strip of baking parchment. Put the chocolate in a small pan. Add 150ml/¼ pint/⅔ cup of the cream and heat very gently until the chocolate has melted. Stir until smooth, then pour into a bowl and leave to cool.

2 Break the chocolate brownies into chunky pieces and scatter these on the bottom of the prepared tin. Pack them down lightly to make a fairly dense base.

3 Whip the remaining cream until it forms peaks, then fold in the white chocolate mixture. Spoon into the tin to cover the layer of brownies, then tap the tin gently on the work surface to level the chocolate mixture. Cover and freeze overnight.

4 Transfer the torte to the refrigerator about 45 minutes before serving, then remove the tin to serve. Decorate with a light dusting of cocoa powder before serving.

Cook's Tips
• If you are unable to find good quality brownies, use a moist chocolate sponge instead.
• Serve with a fresh fruit salad as a foil to the richness. A simple mix of summer fruit topped with a purée made from lightly cooked raspberries is the perfect partner. Or try tropical fruit tossed in a syrup made by dissolving sugar in lemon juice and water, then adding chopped fresh ginger to taste.

Nougat Torte Energy 462Kcal/1929kJ; Protein 8.8g; Carbohydrate 46.7g, of which sugars 38.1g; Fat 28g, of which saturates 14.2g; Cholesterol 134mg; Calcium 119mg; Fibre 0.9g; Sodium 129mg.
White Chocolate Energy 570Kcal/2365kJ; Protein 5.2g; Carbohydrate 31.1g, of which sugars 25.7g; Fat 48.1g, of which saturates 25.6g; Cholesterol 82mg; Calcium 129mg; Fibre 0g; Sodium 154mg.

Soft Fruit & Crushed Meringue Gâteau

This recipe takes five minutes to make but looks and tastes as though a lot of preparation went into the dish. Use a really good vanilla ice cream for the best result.

Serves 6

400g/14oz/3½ cups mixed small
  strawberries, raspberries
  or redcurrants
30ml/2 tbsp icing (confectioners')
  sugar
750ml/1¼ pints/3 cups vanilla
  ice cream
6 meringue nests, or 115g/4oz
  meringue

1 Dampen a 900g/2lb loaf tin (pan) and line it with clear film (plastic wrap). If using strawberries, chop them into small pieces. Put them in a bowl together with the raspberries or redcurrants and icing sugar. Toss until the fruit is beginning to break up, but do not let it become mushy.

2 Put the vanilla ice cream in a large bowl and break it up with a fork. Crumble the meringues into the bowl of ice cream and then add the fruit.

3 Fold all the ingredients together until evenly combined and lightly marbled. Pack into the prepared tin and press down gently to level. Cover and freeze overnight.

4 Transfer the tin to the refrigerator about 30 minutes before serving. To serve, turn out on to a plate and peel away the clear film. Serve in slices.

> **Cook's Tip**
> To make your own meringues, whisk 2 egg whites until stiff. Gradually whisk in 90g/3½oz/½ cup caster (superfine) sugar, then put spoonfuls on to lined baking sheets and cook in the oven, preheated to 150°C/300°F/Gas 2, for 1 hour or until dry.

Brandied Apple Charlotte

Loosely based on a traditional Apple Charlotte, this iced version combines brandy-steeped dried apple with a spicy ricotta cream to make an unusual and very tasty dessert.

Serves 8–10

130g/4½oz/¾ cup dried apples
75ml/5 tbsp brandy
50g/2oz/¼ cup unsalted (sweet)
  butter
115g/4oz/scant ½ cup light
  muscovado (brown) sugar
2.5ml/½ tsp mixed spice
  (apple pie spice)
60ml/4 tbsp water
75g/3oz/½ cup sultanas (golden
  raisins)
300g/11oz Madeira cake, cut
  into 1cm/½in slices
250g/9oz/generous 1 cup
  ricotta cheese
30ml/2 tbsp lemon juice
150ml/¼ pint/⅔ cup double
  (heavy) or whipping cream
icing (confectioners') sugar and
  fresh mint sprigs, to decorate

1 Roughly chop the dried apples, then transfer them to a clean bowl. Pour over the brandy and set aside for about 1 hour until most of the brandy has been absorbed.

2 Melt the butter in a frying pan. Add the sugar and stir over a low heat for 1 minute. Add the mixed spice, water and soaked apples, with any remaining brandy. Cook gently for 5 minutes, stirring occasionally, until the apples are tender. Stir in the sultanas and leave to cool.

3 Use the Madeira slices to line the sides of a 20cm/8in square or 20cm/8in round springform or loose-based cake tin (pan). Place in the freezer while you make the filling.

4 Beat the ricotta in a bowl until it has softened, then stir in the apple mixture and lemon juice. Whip the cream in a separate bowl and fold it in. Spoon the mixture into the lined tin and level the surface. Cover and freeze overnight.

5 Transfer the charlotte to the refrigerator 1 hour before serving. Turn it out on to a serving plate, dust with sugar, and decorate with mint sprigs.

Soft Fruit & Meringue Energy 332Kcal/1397kJ; Protein 6.1g; Carbohydrate 52.4g, of which sugars 51g; Fat 10.8g, of which saturates 7.6g; Cholesterol 30mg; Calcium 141mg; Fibre 0.7g; Sodium 102mg.
Apple Charlotte Energy 373Kcal/1558kJ; Protein 5g; Carbohydrate 40.6g, of which sugars 34g; Fat 20.4g, of which saturates 12.4g; Cholesterol 42mg; Calcium 41mg; Fibre 1.2g; Sodium 152mg.

Mocha, Prune & Armagnac Terrines

A sophisticated iced dessert
for entertaining in style.

Serves 6
115g/4oz/½ cup ready-to-eat
   pitted prunes, chopped
90ml/6 tbsp Armagnac
90g/3½oz/½ cup caster
   (superfine) sugar

150ml/¼ pint/⅔ cup water
45ml/3 tbsp coffee beans
150g/5oz plain (semisweet)
   chocolate, broken into pieces
300ml/½ pint/1¼ cups
   double (heavy) cream
cocoa powder (unsweetened),
   for dusting

1 Put the prunes in a small bowl. Pour over 75ml/5 tbsp of the
Armagnac and leave to soak for at least 3 hours at room
temperature, or overnight in the refrigerator. Line the bases of
six 100ml/3½fl oz/scant ½ cup ramekins with baking parchment.

2 Put the sugar and water in a heavy pan and heat gently until
the sugar dissolves, stirring occasionally. Add the soaked prunes
and any of the Armagnac that remains in the bowl; simmer the
prunes gently in the syrup for 5 minutes.

3 Using a slotted spoon, lift the prunes out of the pan and set
them aside. Add the coffee beans to the syrup and simmer
gently for 5 minutes.

4 Lift out the coffee beans and put about a third of them in a
bowl. Spoon over 120ml/4fl oz/½ cup of the syrup and stir in
the remaining Armagnac.

5 Add the chocolate to the pan containing the remaining syrup
and leave until melted. Whip the cream until it just holds its
shape. Using a large metal spoon, fold the chocolate mixture and
prunes into the cream until just combined. Spoon the mixture
into the lined ramekins, cover and freeze for at least 3 hours.

6 To serve, loosen the edges of the ramekins with a knife then
dip in very hot water for 2 seconds and invert on to serving
plates. Decorate the plates with the coffee bean syrup and a
dusting of cocoa powder.

Double Chocolate Snowball

An ideal party dessert as it
can be prepared ahead and
decorated on the day.

8 eggs
50ml/2fl oz/¼ cup orange-
   flavoured liqueur (optional)

Serves 12–14
350g/12oz plain (semisweet)
   chocolate, chopped
285g/10½oz/1½ cups caster
   (superfine) sugar
275g/10oz/1¼ cups unsalted
   (sweet) butter, diced

For the chocolate cream
200g/7oz good-quality white
   chocolate, broken into pieces
475ml/16fl oz/2 cups double
   (heavy) or whipping cream
30ml/2 tbsp orange-flavoured
   liqueur (optional)

1 Preheat the oven to 180°C/350°F/Gas 4. Line a 1.75 litre/
3 pint/7½ cup round ovenproof bowl with foil, smoothing the
sides. In a bowl over a pan of simmering water, melt the plain
chocolate. Add the sugar and stir until it dissolves. Strain into a
medium bowl. Using an electric mixer at low speed, beat in the
butter, then the eggs, one at a time. Stir in the liqueur, if using,
and pour into the lined bowl. Tap to release large air bubbles.

2 Bake for 1¼–1½ hours until the surface is firm and slightly
risen, but cracked. The centre will set on cooling. Transfer to a
rack to cool. Cover with a plate, then cover completely with
clear film (plastic wrap) and chill overnight. To unmould, remove
the plate and film and invert the mould on to a plate; shake
firmly to release. Peel off foil. Cover until ready to decorate.

3 Work the white chocolate in a food processor to form fine
crumbs. In a small pan, heat 120ml/4fl oz/½ cup of the cream
until just beginning to simmer. With the processor running, pour
in the cream until the chocolate has melted. Strain into a bowl
and cool to room temperature, stirring occasionally.

4 Beat the remaining cream until soft peaks form, add the
liqueur, if using, and beat for 30 seconds or until the cream just
holds its shape. Fold a spoonful of cream into the chocolate
then fold in the remaining cream. Spoon into an icing (pastry)
bag fitted with a star tip and pipe rosettes over the surface.

Iced Lime Cheesecake

This deliciously tangy, iced cheesecake has the advantage of not needing gelatine to set the filling.

Serves 10
175g/6oz almond biscuits (cookies), broken up
65g/2½oz/5 tbsp unsalted (sweet) butter, plus extra for greasing

8 limes
115g/4oz/generous ½ cup caster (superfine) sugar
90ml/6 tbsp water
200g/7oz/scant 1 cup cottage cheese
250g/9oz/generous 1 cup mascarpone
300ml/½ pint/1¼ cups double (heavy) cream

1 Lightly grease the base and sides of a 20cm/8in springform cake tin (pan) and line with baking parchment. Put the biscuits in a strong plastic bag and crush finely with a rolling pin.

2 Melt the butter in a small pan and stir in the biscuit crumbs until evenly combined. Spoon the mixture into the tin and pack down with the back of a spoon. Freeze while making the filling.

3 Finely grate the rind and squeeze the juice from five of the limes. Heat the sugar and water in a small, heavy pan, stirring until the sugar has dissolved. Boil for 2 minutes, without stirring, then remove from the heat. Stir in the lime juice and rind; cool.

4 Press the cottage cheese through a sieve (strainer) into a large bowl. Beat in the mascarpone, then the lime syrup. Lightly whip the cream and fold into the cheese mixture. Pour into a shallow freezer container, cover and freeze until thick.

5 Meanwhile, using a sharp knife, remove all the peel and pith from the remaining limes, then cut the flesh into thin slices. Arrange the slices around the sides of the tin, against the lining.

6 Pour the mixture into the tin and level the surface. Cover with clear film (plastic wrap) and freeze the cheesecake overnight. About 1 hour before serving, transfer the cheesecake to a serving plate and put in the refrigerator to soften slightly.

Elderflower & Lime Yogurt Ice

Fragrant elderflowers have a wonderful flavour, but they are in season for only a very short time. Fortunately, good-quality ready-made elderflower cordial is readily available and combines beautifully with limes to make a lovely iced dessert.

Serves 6
4 egg yolks
50g/2oz/¼ cup caster (superfine) sugar

10ml/2 tsp cornflour (cornstarch)
300ml/½ pint/1¼ cups milk
finely grated rind and juice of 2 limes
150ml/¼ pint/⅔ cup elderflower cordial
200ml/7fl oz/scant 1 cup Greek (US strained plain) yogurt
150ml/¼ pint/⅔ cup double (heavy) cream
grated lime rind, to decorate

1 Whisk the egg yolks in a bowl with the sugar, cornflour and a little of the milk. Pour the remaining milk into a heavy pan, bring it to the boil, then pour it over the yolk mixture, whisking constantly. Return the mixture to the pan and cook over a very gentle heat, stirring constantly until the custard thickens. Do not let it boil or it may curdle.

2 Pour the custard into a bowl and add the lime rind and juice. Pour in the elderflower cordial and mix lightly. Cover the surface of the mixture closely with baking parchment. Leave to cool, then chill until very cold.

3 Whip together the yogurt and cream and fold into the custard. Pour the mixture into a freezer container and freeze for 3–4 hours, beating twice as it thickens. Scoop into individual dishes and return to the freezer until ready to serve.

4 Alternatively, use an ice cream maker. Stir the yogurt and cream into the custard and churn until it thickens. Transfer the yogurt ice into individual dishes and freeze until required.

5 Transfer the yogurt ice to the refrigerator 30 minutes before serving. Decorate with the grated lime rind and serve.

Iced Lime Energy 385Kcal/1602kJ; Protein 6.4g; Carbohydrate 28g, of which sugars 20.5g; Fat 28.1g, of which saturates 17.2g; Cholesterol 69mg; Calcium 71mg; Fibre 0.3g; Sodium 165mg.
Elderflower & Lime Ice Energy 219Kcal/912kJ; Protein 4.3g; Carbohydrate 12.4g, of which sugars 10.9g; Fat 17.7g, of which saturates 10.6g; Cholesterol 37mg; Calcium 125mg; Fibre 0g; Sodium 54mg.

Almond Caramel Custard

Known as crème caramel in France and as flan in Spain, this classic baked custard has been given an unusual twist by adding a hint of almond, rather than vanilla. It tastes wonderful served with strawberries and cream.

Serves 6–8
250g/9oz/1¼ cups granulated sugar
425ml/15fl oz/1¾ cups double (heavy) cream
5ml/1 tsp almond extract
5 large (US extra large) eggs, plus 2 extra yolks

1 Put 175g/6oz/¾ cup of the sugar in a small heavy pan with just enough water to moisten the sugar. Bring to the boil over a high heat, swirling the pan until the sugar has dissolved. Boil for about 5 minutes, without stirring, until the syrup is a dark caramel colour.

2 Working quickly, pour the caramel into a 1 litre/1¾ pint/4 cup soufflé dish. Holding the dish with oven gloves, carefully swirl to coat the base and sides with the caramel. Set aside to cool.

3 Preheat the oven to 160°C/325°F/Gas 3. Put the cream and almond extract in a pan and bring just to the boil over a medium-high heat, stirring. Remove from the heat, cover and cool for 20 minutes.

4 In a bowl, whisk the eggs and egg yolks with the remaining sugar for 2–3 minutes until the mixture is creamy. Whisk in the warm cream and pour into the caramel-lined dish. Cover tightly with foil.

5 Place the dish in a roasting tin (pan) and pour in boiling water to come halfway up the side of the dish. Bake for 40–45 minutes until just set. To test whether it is set, insert a knife near the edge; if it comes out clean, the custard should be ready. Remove the soufflé dish from the tin and leave to cool for at least 30 minutes, then chill overnight.

6 To turn out, run a sharp knife around the edge of the dish. Invert on to a serving plate, then gently lift one edge of the dish, allowing the caramel to escape. Lift off the dish and serve.

Mango & Chocolate Crème Brûlée

Fresh mangoes, topped with a wickedly rich chocolate cream and a layer of crunchy caramel, make a fantastic dessert.

Serves 6
2 ripe mangoes, peeled, stoned (pitted) and chopped
300ml/½ pint/1¼ cups double (heavy) cream
300ml/½ pint/1¼ cups crème fraîche
1 vanilla pod (bean)
115g/4oz plain (semisweet) chocolate, chopped into small pieces
4 egg yolks
15ml/1 tbsp clear honey
90ml/6 tbsp demerara (raw) sugar, for the topping

1 Divide the mangoes among six flameproof dishes set on a baking sheet.

2 Mix the cream, crème fraîche and vanilla pod in a large heatproof bowl. Place the bowl over a pan of barely simmering water.

3 Heat the cream mixture for 10 minutes. Do not let the bowl touch the water or the cream may overheat. Remove the vanilla pod and stir in the chocolate, a few pieces at a time, until melted. When smooth, remove the bowl, but leave the pan of water over the heat.

4 Whisk the egg yolks and clear honey in a second heatproof bowl, then gradually pour in the chocolate cream, whisking constantly. Place over the pan of simmering water and stir constantly until the chocolate custard thickens enough to coat the back of a wooden spoon.

5 Remove from the heat and spoon the custard over the mangoes. Cool, then chill in the refrigerator until set.

6 Preheat the grill (broiler) to high. Sprinkle 15ml/1 tbsp demerara sugar evenly over each dessert and spray lightly with a little water. Grill (broil) briefly, as close to the heat as possible, until the sugar melts and caramelizes. Chill again before serving.

Custard Energy 448Kcal/1864kJ; Protein 5.6g; Carbohydrate 33.6g, of which sugars 33.6g; Fat 33.4g, of which saturates 19.1g; Cholesterol 242mg; Calcium 66mg; Fibre 0g; Sodium 60mg.
Brûlée Energy 670Kcal/2782kJ; Protein 5.2g; Carbohydrate 38.9g, of which sugars 38.4g; Fat 56g, of which saturates 34.6g; Cholesterol 261mg; Calcium 90mg; Fibre 1.8g; Sodium 31mg.

Pear & Gingerbread Sundaes

The best sundaes do not consist solely of ice cream, but are a feast of flavours that melt into each other, rather like a trifle. Poach the pears and chill them well in advance, so that the dessert can be assembled in minutes. As a finishing touch, serve with wafers.

Serves 4
65g/2½oz/5 tbsp light muscovado (brown) sugar
90ml/6 tbsp water
30ml/2 tbsp lemon juice
40g/1½oz/⅓ cup sultanas (golden raisins) or raisins
1.5ml/¼ tsp mixed (apple pie) spice
4 small pears
150g/5oz moist gingerbread or ginger cake
250ml/8fl oz/1 cup vanilla ice cream

1 Heat the sugar and water in a heavy pan until the sugar has dissolved. Add the lemon juice, sultanas or raisins and spice. Peel, quarter and core the pears, then add them to the pan.

2 Cover the pan and simmer very gently for 5–10 minutes until the pears are just tender. Cool the pears in the syrup. Using a slotted spoon, lift them out of the syrup and put them in a bowl. Pour the syrup into a jug (pitcher). Chill both the pears and syrup in the refrigerator.

3 Cut the gingerbread or ginger cake into four pieces and arrange in four glass dishes. Divide the pears among the glasses, then pile vanilla ice cream in the centre of each portion. Pour a little of the syrup over each sundae and serve.

Variation
This extremely quick and easy dessert can be made just as successfully with tart dessert apples. Peel, quarter and core the apples, then cook as for the pears, until just tender. Replace some of the water with clear apple juice to make the apple flavour more intense.

Chocolate Fudge Sundaes

A banana and ice cream treat, highlighted with coffee.

Serves 4
4 scoops each vanilla and coffee ice cream
2 small ripe bananas
whipped cream
toasted flaked (sliced) almonds

For the sauce
50g/2oz/¼ cup soft light brown sugar
120ml/4fl oz/½ cup golden (light corn) syrup
45ml/3 tbsp strong black coffee
5ml/1 tsp ground cinnamon
150g/5oz plain (semisweet) chocolate, chopped into pieces
75ml/2½fl oz/⅓ cup whipping cream
45ml/3 tbsp coffee-flavoured liqueur (optional)

1 Make the sauce. Place the sugar, syrup, coffee and cinnamon in a heavy pan. Bring to the boil, then boil for about 5 minutes, stirring the mixture constantly.

2 Turn off the heat and stir in the chocolate pieces. When the chocolate has melted and the mixture is smooth, stir in the cream and the coffee-flavoured liqueur, if using. Set the sauce aside to cool slightly.

3 Fill four glasses with a scoop each of vanilla and coffee ice cream.

4 Peel the bananas and slice them thinly. Sprinkle the sliced bananas over the ice cream. Pour the warm fudge sauce over the bananas, then top each sundae with a generous swirl of whipped cream. Sprinkle the sundaes with toasted almonds and serve at once.

Cook's Tip
You can make the chocolate sauce ahead of time and reheat it gently, until just warm, when you are ready to make the sundaes. Assemble the sundaes just before serving.

Pear & Gingerbread Energy 404Kcal/1706kJ; Protein 5.2g; Carbohydrate 75.6g, of which sugars 63.7g; Fat 10.3g, of which saturates 3.8g; Cholesterol 15mg; Calcium 125mg; Fibre 4g; Sodium 120mg.
Chocolate Fudge Energy 642Kcal/2690kJ; Protein 5.5g; Carbohydrate 85.9g, of which sugars 84g; Fat 33.1g, of which saturates 20.5g; Cholesterol 64mg; Calcium 115mg; Fibre 1.4g; Sodium 132mg.

Tiramisu in Chocolate Cups

The Italian favourite served in an elegant new way.

Serves 6
1 egg yolk
30ml/2 tbsp caster (superfine) sugar
2.5ml/½ tsp vanilla extract
250g/9oz/generous 1 cup mascarpone cheese
120ml/4fl oz/½ cup strong black coffee
15ml/1 tbsp cocoa powder (unsweetened), plus extra for dusting
30ml/2 tbsp coffee liqueur
16 amaretti

For the chocolate cups
175g/6oz plain (semisweet) chocolate, chopped
25g/1oz/2 tbsp unsalted (sweet) butter

1 Make the chocolate cups. Cut out six 15cm/6in rounds of baking parchment. Melt the chocolate with the butter in a heatproof bowl over a pan of simmering water. Stir until smooth, then spread a spoonful of the chocolate mixture over each circle, to within 2cm/¾in of the edge.

2 Carefully lift each paper round and drape it over an upturned teacup or ramekin so that the edges curve into frills. Leave until completely set, then carefully peel away the paper.

3 Make the filling. Using a hand-held electric mixer, beat the egg yolk and sugar in a bowl until smooth, then stir in the vanilla extract. Soften the mascarpone if necessary, then stir it into the egg yolk mixture. Beat until smooth.

4 In a separate bowl, mix the coffee, cocoa and liqueur. Break up the amaretti roughly, then stir them into the mixture.

5 Place the chocolate cups on individual plates. Divide half the amaretti mixture among them, then spoon over half the mascarpone mixture.

6 Spoon over the remaining amaretti mixture (including any free liquid), top with the rest of the mascarpone mixture and dust lightly with cocoa. Chill for 30 minutes before serving.

Chocolate Blancmange

An old-fashioned dessert that deserves a revival. Serve with pouring cream for a touch of luxury.

Serves 4
60ml/4 tbsp cornflour (cornstarch)
600ml/1 pint/2½ cups milk
45ml/3 tbsp sugar
50–115g/2–4oz plain (semisweet) chocolate, chopped
few drops of vanilla extract
white and plain (semisweet) chocolate curls, to decorate

1 Rinse a 750ml/1¼ pint/3 cup fluted mould with cold water and leave it upside down to drain. Blend the cornflour to a smooth paste with a little of the milk in a medium bowl.

2 Bring the remaining milk to the boil, preferably in a non-stick pan, then pour on to the blended paste, stirring constantly, until smooth in consistency.

3 Pour all the milk back into the pan and bring slowly to the boil over a low heat, stirring constantly until the mixture boils and thickens. Remove the pan from the heat, then add the sugar, chopped chocolate and vanilla extract and stir until the sauce is smooth, all the sugar has dissolved and the chocolate pieces have melted completely.

4 Carefully pour the chocolate mixture into the mould, cover the top closely with dampened baking parchment (to prevent the formation of a skin) and leave in a cool place for several hours to set.

5 To unmould the blancmange, place a large serving plate upside down on top of the mould. Holding the plate and mould firmly together, turn them both over. Give both plate and mould a gentle but firm shake to loosen the blancmange, then carefully lift off the mould.

6 To serve, sprinkle the chocolate curls over the top.

Blancmange Energy 230Kcal/975kJ; Protein 5.9g; Carbohydrate 40.6g, of which sugars 26.6g; Fat 6.2g, of which saturates 3.7g; Cholesterol 10mg; Calcium 192mg; Fibre 0.3g; Sodium 74mg.
Tiramisu Energy 351Kcal/1469kJ; Protein 6.9g; Carbohydrate 34.5g, of which sugars 29.6g; Fat 20.4g, of which saturates 12.1g; Cholesterol 62mg; Calcium 33mg; Fibre 1.2g; Sodium 86mg.

Chocolate Cones with Apricot Sauce

Glamorous chocolate cones with a luxurious filling.

Serves 6

250g/9oz plain (semisweet) chocolate, chopped into small pieces
350g/12oz/1½ cups ricotta cheese
45ml/3 tbsp double (heavy) cream
30ml/2 tbsp brandy
30ml/2 tbsp icing (confectioners') sugar
finely grated rind of 1 lemon
pared strips of lemon rind, to decorate

For the sauce
175g/6oz/⅔ cup apricot jam
45ml/3 tbsp lemon juice

1 Cut twelve 10cm/4in double thickness rounds from baking parchment and shape each into a cone. Secure in place with masking tape.

2 Melt the chocolate in a bowl over a pan of simmering water. Cool slightly, then spoon a little into each cone, swirling and brushing it to coat the paper evenly.

3 Support each cone point downwards in a cup or glass held on its side, to keep it level. Leave in a cool place until the cones are completely set. Unless it is a very hot day, do not put the cones in the refrigerator, as this may spoil their appearance.

4 Make the sauce. Combine the apricot jam and lemon juice in a small pan. Place over a gentle heat until melted, stirring occasionally, then press through a sieve (strainer) into a small bowl. Set aside to cool.

5 Beat the ricotta cheese in a bowl until softened, then beat in the cream, brandy and icing sugar. Stir in the grated lemon rind. Spoon the mixture into a piping (pastry) bag. Fill the cones, then carefully peel off the baking parchment.

6 Spoon a pool of apricot sauce on to six dessert plates. Arrange the cones in pairs on the plates. Decorate with a scattering of pared lemon rind strips and serve immediately.

Chocolate Vanilla Timbales

These elegantly turned-out timbales look particularly impressive if they are set in fluted moulds. It's worth investing in some.

Serves 6

350ml/12fl oz/1½ cups semi-skimmed (low-fat) milk
30ml/2 tbsp cocoa powder (unsweetened), plus extra for dusting
2 eggs
10ml/2 tsp vanilla extract
45ml/3 tbsp caster (superfine) sugar
15ml/1 tbsp/1 sachet powdered gelatine
45ml/3 tbsp hot water
fresh mint sprigs, to decorate

For the sauce
115g/4oz/½ cup light Greek (US strained plain) yogurt
25ml/1½ tbsp vanilla extract

1 Place the milk and cocoa in a pan and stir until the milk is boiling. Separate the eggs and beat the egg yolks with the vanilla extract and sugar in a bowl, until the mixture is pale and smooth. Gradually pour in the chocolate milk, beating well.

2 Return the mixture to the pan and stir constantly over a gentle heat, without boiling, until it is slightly thickened and smooth in consistency.

3 Remove the pan from the heat. Pour the gelatine into the hot water and stir until it is completely dissolved, then quickly stir it into the milk mixture. Put this mixture aside and allow it to cool until almost setting.

4 Whisk the egg whites until they hold soft peaks. Fold the egg whites quickly into the milk mixture. Spoon the timbale mixture into six individual moulds and chill them until set.

5 To serve, run a knife around the edge, dip the moulds quickly into hot water and turn out on to serving plates. For the sauce, stir together the yogurt and vanilla extract and spoon on to the plates next to the timbales. Lightly dust with cocoa and decorate with mint sprigs.

Cones Energy 461Kcal/1932kJ; Protein 7.8g; Carbohydrate 53.8g, of which sugars 53.4g; Fat 24.2g, of which saturates 14.8g; Cholesterol 37mg; Calcium 24mg; Fibre 1.1g; Sodium 13mg.
Timbales Energy 89Kcal/372kJ; Protein 6.2g; Carbohydrate 3.7g, of which sugars 3.1g; Fat 5.9g, of which saturates 2.8g; Cholesterol 67mg; Calcium 115mg; Fibre 0.6g; Sodium 110mg.

Orange & Yogurt Ice

With this low-fat ice, you can indulge in a dessert without feeling too guilty.

Serves 6
90ml/6 tbsp water
10ml/2 tsp powdered gelatine
115g/4oz/generous ½ cup caster (superfine) sugar

250ml/8fl oz/1 cup freshly squeezed orange juice from a carton or bottle
500ml/17fl oz/generous 2 cups bio yogurt
cones or meringue nests, blueberries and fresh mint sprigs, to serve

1 Put 30ml/2 tbsp of the water in a small bowl and sprinkle the powdered gelatine over the top. Set aside until spongy. Meanwhile, put the sugar in a small pan, add the remaining water and heat through gently until the sugar has dissolved.

2 Remove the pan from the heat, add the gelatine and stir until completely dissolved. Cool, stir in the orange juice and chill for 15–30 minutes.

3 Spoon the yogurt into a bowl, gradually add the chilled orange juice mixture and mix well. Pour the mixture into a freezer container. Freeze for 6 hours or until firm, beating twice with a fork or in a food processor to break up the ice crystals.

4 Alternatively, use an ice cream maker. Freeze the mixture until starting to thicken. Switch off the machine, remove the paddle, if necessary, add the yogurt and mix well. Replace the paddle and continue to churn the ice cream for 15–20 minutes until thick. Scrape it into a freezer container and freeze until firm.

5 Scoop the yogurt ice into cones or meringue nests and decorate with blueberries and mint.

> **Cook's Tip**
> Meringue nests are not difficult to make, but if you do not have the time, bought ones are a perfectly acceptable alternative.

Frozen Strawberry Mousse Cake

Children will love this pretty dessert – it tastes just like an ice cream.

Serves 4–6
425g/15oz can strawberries in syrup
15ml/1 tbsp/1 sachet powdered gelatine

6 trifle sponge cakes
45ml/3 tbsp strawberry jam
200ml/7fl oz/scant 1 cup crème fraîche
200ml/7fl oz/⅞ cup whipped cream, to decorate

1 Strain the syrup from the strawberries into a large heatproof bowl. Sprinkle over the gelatine and stir well. Stand the bowl in a pan of hot water and stir until the gelatine has dissolved.

2 Leave to cool, then chill for just under 1 hour, until beginning to set. Meanwhile, cut the sponge cakes in half lengthways and spread the cut surfaces with the strawberry jam.

3 Carefully whisk the crème fraîche into the strawberry jelly, then whisk in the canned strawberries. Line a deep, 20cm/8in loose-based cake tin (pan) with baking parchment.

4 Pour half the strawberry mousse mixture into the tin, arrange the sponge cakes over the surface, and then spoon over the remaining mousse mixture, pushing down any sponge cakes that rise up.

5 Freeze for 1–2 hours until the mousse is firm. Remove the cake from the tin and carefully peel away the lining paper. Transfer to a serving plate. Decorate the mousse with whirls of whipped cream and a few strawberry leaves and a fresh strawberry, if they are available.

> **Variation**
> Replace the crème fraîche with a mix of lightly whipped double (heavy) cream and low-fat yogurt for a less rich cake.

Pear & Hazelnut Meringue Torte

This stunning dessert will raise gasps of admiration.

Serves 8–10
175g/6oz/¾ cup granulated sugar
1 vanilla pod (bean), split
475ml/16fl oz/2 cups water
4 ripe pears, peeled, halved and cored
30ml/2 tbsp hazelnut- or pear-flavoured liqueur
150g/5oz/1¼ cups hazelnuts, toasted
6 egg whites

pinch of salt
350g/12oz/3 cups icing (confectioners') sugar
5ml/1 tsp vanilla extract
50g/2oz plain (semisweet) chocolate, melted

For the chocolate cream
275g/10oz plain (semisweet) chocolate, chopped into small pieces
475ml/16fl oz/2 cups whipping cream
60ml/4 tbsp hazelnut- or pear-flavoured liqueur

1 In a pan large enough to hold the pears in a single layer, combine the sugar, vanilla pod and water. Over a high heat, bring to the boil, stirring until the sugar dissolves. Lower the heat, add the pears to the syrup, cover and simmer gently for 12–15 minutes until tender. Remove the pan from the heat and allow the pears to cool in their poaching liquid. Carefully lift the pears out of the liquid and drain on kitchen paper. Transfer them to a plate, sprinkle with liqueur, cover and chill overnight.

2 Preheat the oven to 180°C/350°F/Gas 4. With a pencil, draw a 23cm/9in circle on each of two sheets of baking parchment. Turn the paper over on to two baking sheets (so that the pencil marks are underneath). Grind the toasted hazelnuts.

3 In a large bowl, beat the whites with a hand-held electric mixer until frothy. Add the salt and beat on high speed until soft peaks form. Reduce the mixer speed and gradually add the icing sugar, beating well after each addition until all the sugar has been added and the whites are stiff and glossy. Gently fold in the nuts and vanilla extract and spoon the meringue on to the circles on the baking sheets, smoothing the top and sides.

4 Bake for 1 hour until the tops are dry and firm. Turn off the oven and cool in the oven for 2–3 hours or overnight, until dry.

5 Make the chocolate cream. Melt the chocolate in a heatproof bowl set over a pan of simmering water and stir until melted and smooth. Cool to room temperature. Whip the cream in a bowl to soft peaks. Quickly fold the cream into the chocolate; fold in the liqueur. Spoon about one-third of the chocolate cream into an icing (pastry) bag fitted with a star tip. Set aside.

6 Thinly slice each pear half lengthways. Place one meringue layer on a serving plate. Spread with half the chocolate cream and arrange half the pears on top. Pipe rosettes around edge.

7 Top with the second meringue layer, spread with the remaining chocolate cream and arrange the remaining pear slices on top. Pipe a border of rosettes around the edge. Spoon the melted chocolate into a small paper cone and drizzle the chocolate over the pears. Chill for at least 1 hour before serving.

Raspberry Meringue Gâteau

A rich hazelnut meringue sandwiched with whipped cream and raspberries is the ultimate in elegance.

Serves 6
4 egg whites
225g/8oz/1 cup caster (superfine) sugar
a few drops of vanilla extract
5ml/1 tsp distilled malt vinegar
115g/4oz/1 cup roasted and chopped hazelnuts, ground

300ml/½ pint/1¼ cups double (heavy) cream
350g/12oz/2 cups raspberries
icing (confectioners') sugar, for dusting
raspberries and mint sprigs, to decorate

For the sauce
225g/8oz/1⅓ cups raspberries
45–60ml/3–4 tbsp icing (confectioners') sugar, sifted
15ml/1 tbsp orange liqueur

1 Preheat the oven to 180°C/350°F/Gas 4. Grease two 20cm/8in sandwich tins (layer cake pans) and line the bases with baking parchment.

2 Whisk the egg whites in a large bowl until they hold stiff peaks, then gradually whisk in the caster sugar a tablespoon at a time, whisking well after each addition. Continue whisking the meringue mixture for a minute or two until very stiff, then fold in the vanilla extract, vinegar and ground hazelnuts.

3 Divide the meringue mixture between the prepared tins and spread level. Bake for 50–60 minutes, until crisp. Remove the meringues from the tins and leave them to cool on a wire rack.

4 Meanwhile, make the sauce. Process the raspberries with the icing sugar and liqueur in a blender or food processor, then press through a sieve (strainer) to remove seeds. Chill the sauce.

5 Whip the cream until it forms soft peaks, then gently fold in the raspberries. Sandwich the meringue rounds together with the raspberry cream.

6 Dust the top of the gâteau with icing sugar. Decorate with mint sprigs and serve with the raspberry sauce.

Torte Energy 706Kcal/2960kJ; Protein 6.9g; Carbohydrate 86.1g, of which sugars 85.5g; Fat 37.4g, of which saturates 17.9g; Cholesterol 52mg; Calcium 97mg; Fibre 3.1g; Sodium 64mg.
Gâteau Energy 354Kcal/1477kJ; Protein 4.2g; Carbohydrate 32.4g, of which sugars 32.2g; Fat 23.6g, of which saturates 10.6g; Cholesterol 41mg; Calcium 60mg; Fibre 2.2g; Sodium 35mg.

Chocolate Tiramisu Tart

This tart has an utterly delicious creamy filling.

Serves 12–16
115g/4oz/½ cup butter
15ml/1 tbsp coffee-flavoured liqueur
175g/6oz/1½ cups plain
    (all-purpose) flour
25g/1oz/¼ cup cocoa powder
    (unsweetened), plus extra for
    dusting
25g/1oz/¼ cup icing
    (confectioners') sugar
pinch of salt
2.5ml/½ tsp vanilla extract

For the chocolate layer
350ml/12fl oz/1½ cups double
(heavy) cream
15ml/1 tbsp golden (light corn) syrup
115g/4oz plain (semisweet)
    chocolate, chopped into pieces
25g/1oz/2 tbsp unsalted (sweet)
    butter, cut into small pieces
30ml/2 tbsp coffee-flavoured liqueur

For the filling
250ml/8fl oz/1 cup whipping cream
350g/12oz/1½ cups mascarpone,
    at room temperature
45ml/3 tbsp icing sugar
45ml/3 tbsp cold espresso or
    strong black coffee
45ml/3 tbsp coffee-flavoured liqueur
90g/3½oz plain (semisweet)
    chocolate, grated

1 Make the pastry. Grease a 23cm/9in springform tin (pan). Heat the butter and liqueur until the butter melts. Sift the flour, cocoa, icing sugar and salt into a bowl. Remove the butter mixture from the heat, stir in the vanilla and stir into the flour mixture until soft dough forms. Knead until smooth. Press on to the base and up the sides of the tin. Prick the dough. Chill for 40 minutes. Preheat the oven to 190°C/375°F/Gas 5. Bake the pastry case for 8–10 minutes. If the pastry puffs up, prick it with a fork and bake for 2–3 minutes more until set. Cool in the tin on a rack.

2 Mix the cream and syrup in a pan. Bring to a boil over medium heat. Off the heat, stir in the chocolate until melted. Beat in the butter and liqueur and pour into the pastry case. Cool and chill.

3 Make the filling. In one bowl, whip the cream until soft peaks form; in another, beat the cheese until soft, then beat in icing sugar until smooth. Add the coffee, liqueur, cream and chocolate. Spoon into the pastry case, on top of the chocolate layer. Level the surface. Chill until ready to serve, dusted with cocoa.

Chocolate Truffle Tart

A dreamy chilled tart with a chocolate flavoured pastry case and a luscious filling, laced with brandy.

Serves 12
115g/4oz/1 cup plain
    (all-purpose) flour
40g/1¼oz/⅓ cup cocoa powder
    (unsweetened)
50g/2oz/¼ cup caster
    (superfine) sugar
2.5ml/½ tsp salt
115g/4oz/½ cup unsalted (sweet)
    butter, cut into pieces
1 egg yolk

15–30ml/1–2 tbsp iced water
25g/1oz good-quality white or
    milk chocolate, melted
whipped cream for serving
    (optional)

For the truffle filling
350ml/12fl oz/1½ cups double
    (heavy) cream
350g/12oz fine plain
    (bittersweet) chocolate,
    chopped
50g/2oz/4 tbsp unsalted (sweet)
    butter, cut into small pieces
30ml/2 tbsp brandy or liqueur

1 Make the pastry. Sift the flour and cocoa into a bowl. In a food processor fitted with a metal blade, process the flour mixture with the sugar and salt. Add the butter and process for a further 15–20 seconds, until the mixture resembles coarse breadcrumbs.

2 Lightly beat the yolk with the iced water in a bowl. Add to the flour mixture and pulse until the dough begins to stick together. Turn out the dough on to a sheet of clear film (plastic wrap). Use the film to help shape the dough into a flat disc. Wrap tightly. Chill for 1–2 hours, until firm.

3 Lightly grease a 23cm/9in flan tin (tart pan) with a removable base. Let the dough soften briefly, then roll it out between sheets of baking parchment or clear film (plastic wrap) to a 28cm/11in round, about 5mm/¼in thick. Peel off the top sheet and invert the dough into the tart tin. Remove the bottom sheet. Ease the dough into the tin. Prick with a fork. Chill for 1 hour.

4 Preheat the oven to 180°C/350°F/Gas 4. Line the tart with foil or baking parchment; fill with baking beans. Bake blind for 5–7 minutes. Lift out the foil with the beans, return the pastry case to the oven and bake for a further 5–7 minutes, until the pastry is just set. Cool completely in the tin on a rack.

5 Make the filling. In a medium pan, bring the cream to the boil over a medium heat. Remove the pan from the heat and stir in the chocolate until melted and smooth. Stir in the butter and brandy or liqueur. Strain into the prepared tart shell, tilting the tin slightly to level the surface. Do not touch the surface of the filling or it will spoil the glossy finish.

6 Spoon the melted chocolate into a paper piping (pastry) bag and cut off the tip. Drop rounds of chocolate over the surface of the tart and use a skewer or cocktail stick (toothpick) to draw a point gently through the chocolate to produce a marbled effect. Chill for 2–3 hours, until set.

7 Just before serving, allow the tart to soften slightly at room temperature, then serve with whipped cream, if you like.

Tiramisu Energy 399Kcal/1657kJ; Protein 4.8g; Carbohydrate 24.4g, of which sugars 15.8g; Fat 30.9g, of which saturates 20.4g; Cholesterol 60mg; Calcium 49mg; Fibre 0.9g; Sodium 86mg.
Truffle Tart Energy 474Kcal/1969kJ; Protein 3.7g; Carbohydrate 32.5g, of which sugars 24.6g; Fat 36.8g, of which saturates 22.6g; Cholesterol 88mg; Calcium 48mg; Fibre 1.4g; Sodium 117mg.

White Chocolate & Mango Cream Tart

A rich, exotic tart designed to tantalize the taste buds.

Serves 8

175g/6oz/1½ cups plain
  (all-purpose) flour
75g/3oz/1 cup sweetened,
  desiccated (dry unsweetened
  shredded) coconut
115g/4oz/½ cup butter, softened
30ml/2 tbsp caster (superfine) sugar
2 egg yolks
2.5ml/½ tsp almond extract
120ml/4fl oz/½ cup whipping
  cream, whipped to soft peaks

1 large mango, peeled and sliced
whipped cream and toasted
  almonds, to decorate

For the filling

150g/5oz good-quality white
  chocolate, chopped finely
120ml/4fl oz/½ cup whipping
  cream or double (heavy) cream
75ml/5 tbsp cornflour (cornstarch)
15ml/1 tbsp plain
  (all-purpose) flour
50g/2oz/¼ cup granulated sugar
350ml/12fl oz/1½ cups milk
5 egg yolks

1 Beat the flour, coconut, butter, sugar, egg yolks and almond extract in a bowl to form a soft dough. Grease a 23cm/9in flan tin (tart pan) with a removable base and press the pastry into the tin to line. Prick the base with a fork. Chill for 30 minutes.

2 Preheat the oven to 180°C/350°F/Gas 4. Line the pastry case with baking parchment; fill with baking beans and bake blind for 10 minutes. Remove the paper and beans and bake for a further 5–7 minutes, until golden. Cool in the tin on a wire rack.

3 Make the filling. In a small pan over a low heat, melt the white chocolate with the cream, stirring until smooth. Combine the cornflour, plain flour and sugar in another pan. Gradually stir in the milk and cook gently, stirring constantly, until thickened.

4 Beat the egg yolks in a small bowl. Slowly stir in some of the hot milk mixture. Return the yolk mixture to the rest of the sauce in the pan, stirring. Bring to a gentle boil, stirring, until thickened. Stir in the melted chocolate. Cool, then fold in the whipped cream. Spoon half the custard into the pastry case and arrange the mango on top. Cover with the rest of the custard. Remove from the tin and decorate with piped cream and nuts.

Chocolate Pecan Torte

A luscious chocolate cake, topped with chocolate-glazed pecan nuts, makes a memorable dessert.

Serves 16

200g/7oz dark (bittersweet) or
  plain (semisweet) chocolate,
  chopped into small pieces
150g/5oz/10 tbsp unsalted
  (sweet) butter, cut into pieces,
  plus extra for greasing
4 eggs
90g/3½oz/½ cup caster
  (superfine) sugar

10ml/2 tsp vanilla extract
115g/4oz/1 cup ground pecan
  nuts
10ml/2 tsp ground cinnamon
24 toasted pecan nut halves, to
  decorate

For the glaze

115g/4oz dark (bittersweet) or
  plain (semisweet) chocolate,
  chopped into small pieces
50g/2oz/¼ cup unsalted (sweet)
  butter, cut into pieces
30ml/2 tbsp clear honey
pinch of ground cinnamon

1 Preheat the oven to 180°C/350°F/Gas 4. Grease a 20cm/8in springform tin (pan); line with baking parchment. Wrap the tin in foil to prevent water from seeping in. Melt the chocolate and butter, stirring until smooth. Beat the eggs, sugar and vanilla in a mixing bowl until the mixture is frothy. Stir in the melted chocolate, nuts and cinnamon. Pour into the tin.

2 Place the tin in a roasting pan. Pour in boiling water to come 2cm/¾in up the side of the springform tin. Bake for 25–30 minutes, until the edge of the cake is set but the centre is still soft. Remove the tin from the water bath and lift off the foil. Cool the cake in the tin on a wire rack.

3 Make the glaze. Heat all the ingredients in a small pan until melted, stirring until smooth. Remove from the heat. Half-dip the toasted pecan halves in the glaze and place on a baking sheet lined with baking parchment until set.

4 Remove the cake from the tin, place on the rack and pour the remaining glaze over. Decorate the outside of the torte with the chocolate-dipped pecans and leave to set. Transfer to a plate when ready to serve, and slice into thin wedges.

Choc. & Mango Energy 802Kcal/3336kJ; Protein 12.3g; Carbohydrate 57.3g, of which sugars 30.3g; Fat 59.8g, of which saturates 41.9g; Cholesterol 217mg; Calcium 256mg; Fibre 3.1g; Sodium 195mg.
Chocolate Pecan Torte Energy 308Kcal/1282kJ; Protein 3.6g; Carbohydrate 20.5g, of which sugars 20.1g; Fat 24.2g, of which saturates 10.8g; Cholesterol 75mg; Calcium 25mg; Fibre 1g; Sodium 95mg.

Hot Ice Cream Fritters

Deep-fried ice cream may seem a contradiction in terms, but once you've made these crisp fritters, you'll be converted! The secret is to encase the ice cream thoroughly in two layers of sweet cookie crumbs. This will turn crisp and golden during frying, and the ice cream inside will melt only slightly.

Serves 4
750ml/1¼ pints/3 cups firm vanilla ice cream
115g/4oz amaretti
115g/4oz/2 cups fresh brown breadcrumbs
1 egg
45g/1¾oz/3 tbsp plain (all-purpose) flour
oil, for deep frying

For the caramel sauce
115g/4oz/generous ½ cup caster (superfine) sugar
150ml/¼ pint/⅔ cup water
150ml/¼ pint/⅔ cup double (heavy) cream

1 Line a baking sheet with baking parchment and put it in the freezer for 15 minutes, at the same time removing the ice cream from the freezer to soften slightly. Scoop about 12 balls of ice cream, making them as round as possible, and place them on the lined baking sheet. Freeze for at least 1 hour, until firm.

2 Meanwhile, put the amaretti in a strong plastic bag and crush with a rolling pin. Turn into a bowl and add the breadcrumbs. Mix well, and then transfer half the mixture to a plate. Beat the egg in a shallow dish. Sprinkle the flour on to a second plate.

3 Using cool hands, and working very quickly, roll each ice cream ball in the flour, then dip in the beaten egg until coated. Roll the balls in the mixed crumbs until completely covered. Return the coated ice cream balls to the baking sheet and freeze for at least 1 hour more.

4 Repeat the process, using the remaining flour, egg and mixed crumbs so that each ball has an additional coating. Return the ice cream balls to the freezer for at least 4 hours, preferably overnight, to firm up.

5 Make the sauce. Heat the sugar and water in a small, heavy pan, stirring occasionally, until the sugar has dissolved. Bring to the boil and boil the syrup for about 10 minutes without stirring until deep golden. Immediately immerse the base of the pan in a bowl of cold water to prevent the syrup from cooking any more.

6 Pour the cream into the syrup and return the pan to the heat. Stir until the sauce is smooth. Set aside while you fry the ice cream balls.

7 Pour oil into a heavy pan to a depth of 7.5cm/3in. Heat to 185°C/365°F or until a cube of bread added to the oil browns in 30 seconds. Add several of the ice cream balls and fry for about 1 minute until the coating on each is golden. Drain on kitchen paper and quickly cook the remainder in the same way. Serve the fritters with the caramel sauce.

Toasted Marzipan Parcels with Plums

Melting ice cream, encased in lightly toasted marzipan, makes an irresistible dessert for anyone who likes the flavour of almonds. Lightly poached apricots, cherries, apples or pears can be used instead of the plums.

Serves 4
400g/14oz golden marzipan
icing (confectioners') sugar, for dusting
250ml/8fl oz/1 cup almond, ginger or vanilla ice cream

For the plum compote
3 red plums, about 250g/9oz
25g/1oz/2 tbsp caster (superfine) sugar
75ml/5 tbsp water

1 Roll out the marzipan on a surface lightly dusted with sifted icing sugar to a 45 x 23cm/18 x 9in rectangle. Stamp out eight rounds using a plain 12cm/4½in cookie cutter.

2 Place a spoonful of the ice cream in the centre of one of the circles. Bring the marzipan up over the ice cream and press the edges together to completely encase it.

3 Crimp the edges with your fingers. Transfer to a small baking sheet and freeze. Fill and shape the remaining parcels in the same way and freeze overnight.

4 Make the plum compote. Cut the plums in half, remove the stones (pits), then cut each half into two wedges. Heat the sugar and water in a heavy pan, stirring occasionally, until the sugar has completely dissolved.

5 Add the plums and cook very gently for 5 minutes or until they have softened but retain their shape. Test with the tip of a sharp knife – the flesh of the plums should be just tender.

6 Preheat the grill (broiler) to high. Place the marzipan parcels on the grill rack and cook for 1–2 minutes, watching closely, until the crimped edge of the marzipan is lightly browned. Transfer the parcels to serving plates and serve with the warm plum compote.

Parcels Energy 547Kcal/2307kJ; Protein 8g; Carbohydrate 92g, of which sugars 91.3g; Fat 18.1g, of which saturates 4.9g; Cholesterol 15mg; Calcium 140mg; Fibre 2.9g; Sodium 59mg.
Fritters Energy 1064Kcal/4453kJ; Protein 15.1g; Carbohydrate 121.6g, of which sugars 77g; Fat 58.6g, of which saturates 28.1g; Cholesterol 145mg; Calcium 319mg; Fibre 1.4g; Sodium 454mg.

Ice Cream with Hot Cherry Sauce

Hot cherry sauce transforms ice cream into a delicious dessert for any occasion. Serve immediately to ensure that the sauce is still warm to the taste.

Serves 4

425g/15oz can pitted black cherries in juice
10ml/2 tsp cornflour (cornstarch)
finely grated rind of 1 lemon, plus 10ml/2 tsp juice
15ml/1 tbsp caster (superfine) sugar
2.5ml/½ tsp ground cinnamon
30ml/2 tbsp brandy or kirsch (optional)
400ml/14fl oz/1⅔ cups dark (bittersweet) chocolate ice cream
400ml/14fl oz/1⅔ cups classic vanilla ice cream
drinking chocolate powder, for dusting

1 Drain the cherries, reserving the canned juice. Spoon the cornflour into a small pan and blend to a paste with a little of the reserved juice.

2 Stir in the remaining canned juice with the lemon rind and juice, sugar and cinnamon. Bring to the boil, stirring, until smooth and glossy.

3 Add the cherries, with the brandy or kirsch, if using. Stir gently, then cook for 1 minute.

4 Scoop the chocolate and vanilla ice cream into shallow dishes. Spoon the sauce around, dust with drinking chocolate powder and serve.

Variation
The hot cherry sauce also makes a delicious filling for pancakes. For a speedy dessert, use heated, ready-made sweet pancakes – just spread a little sauce in the centre of each pancake and fold into a triangle shape or roll up. Then arrange in a serving dish and spoon the rest of the sauce over the top. Finish with spoonfuls of thick yogurt or whipped cream.

Prune Beignets in Chocolate Sauce

Combining soft-textured prunes with a crisp batter coating works brilliantly! The rich chocolate sauce is the perfect finishing touch.

Serves 4

75g/3oz/⅔ cup plain (all-purpose) flour
45ml/3 tbsp ground almonds
45ml/3 tbsp oil or melted butter
1 egg white
60ml/4 tbsp water
oil, for deep frying
175g/6oz/1 cup ready-to-eat pitted prunes
45ml/3 tbsp vanilla sugar
15ml/1 tbsp cocoa powder (unsweetened)

For the sauce
200g/7oz milk chocolate, chopped into small pieces
120ml/4fl oz/½ cup crème fraîche
30ml/2 tbsp Armagnac or brandy

1 Make the sauce. Melt the chocolate in a bowl over a pan of hot water. Remove from the heat, stir in the crème fraîche until smooth, then add the Armagnac or brandy. Replace the bowl over the water, off the heat, so that the sauce stays warm.

2 Beat the flour, almonds, oil or butter and egg white in a bowl, then beat in enough of the water to make a thick batter.

3 Heat the oil for deep frying to 180°C/350°F or until a cube of dried bread browns in 30–45 seconds. Dip the prunes into the batter and fry a few at a time until the beignets rise to the surface and are golden brown. Remove each batch of beignets with a slotted spoon, drain on kitchen paper and keep hot.

4 Mix the vanilla sugar and cocoa in a bowl or stout paper bag, add the drained beignets and toss well to coat. Serve in individual bowls, with the chocolate sauce poured over the top.

Cook's Tip
Vanilla sugar is available from good food stores, but it's easy to make your own: simply store a vanilla pod in a jar of sugar for a few weeks until the sugar has taken on the vanilla flavour.

Ice Cream Energy 529Kcal/2213kJ; Protein 8.4g; Carbohydrate 59.5g, of which sugars 57g; Fat 30.2g, of which saturates 18.1g; Cholesterol 0mg; Calcium 218mg; Fibre 0.7g; Sodium 130mg.
Beignets Energy 727Kcal/3039kJ; Protein 11.3g; Carbohydrate 71.7g, of which sugars 56.5g; Fat 44.1g, of which saturates 24.2g; Cholesterol 69mg; Calcium 209mg; Fibre 4.8g; Sodium 176mg.

Ice Cream Bombes with Hot Sauce

These individual ice cream bombes, with a surprise vanilla and chocolate-chip centre, are served with a hot toffee cream sauce to make a truly indulgent dessert.

Serves 6

1 litre/1¾ pints/4 cups soft-scoop chocolate ice cream
475ml/16fl oz/2 cups soft-scoop vanilla ice cream
50g/2oz/⅓ cup plain (semisweet) chocolate chips
115g/4oz toffees
75ml/5 tbsp double (heavy) cream

1 Divide the chocolate ice cream equally among six small cups. Push it roughly to the base and up the sides, leaving a small cup-shaped dip in the middle. Put them in the freezer and leave for 45 minutes. Take the cups out again and smooth the ice cream in each to make cup shapes with hollow centres. Return to the freezer.

2 Put the vanilla ice cream in a small bowl and break it up slightly with a spoon. Stir in the chocolate chips and use this mixture to fill the hollows in the cups of chocolate ice cream. Smooth the tops, then cover the cups with clear film (plastic wrap), return to the freezer and leave overnight.

3 Melt the toffees with the cream in a small pan over a very low heat, stirring constantly until smooth, warm and creamy.

4 Turn out the bombes on to individual plates and pour the toffee sauce over the top. Serve immediately.

Cook's Tips
• To make it easier to unmould the bombes, dip them briefly in hot water, then turn out immediately on to serving plates. If you wish, you can return the unmoulded bombes to the freezer for about 10 minutes to firm up.
• Serve with crisp little biscuits (cookies) for a crunchy contrast.

Summer Berries in Warm Sabayon Glaze

This luxurious combination of summer berries under a light and fluffy alcoholic sauce is lightly cooked to form a crisp, caramelized topping.

Serves 4

450g/1lb/4 cups mixed summer berries, or soft fruit
4 egg yolks
50g/2oz/¼ cup vanilla sugar or caster (superfine) sugar
120ml/4fl oz/½ cup orange liqueur, or a white dessert wine
a little icing (confectioners') sugar, sifted, and mint leaves, to decorate (optional)

1 Arrange the fruit in four individual heatproof dishes. Preheat the grill (broiler).

2 Whisk the egg yolks in a large heatproof bowl with the sugar and liqueur or wine.

3 Place the bowl containing the egg yolks, sugar and liqueur or wine over a pan of hot water and whisk constantly until the mixture is thick, fluffy and pale.

4 Pour equal quantities of the sauce over the fruit in each individual dish. Place under the grill for 1–2 minutes until just turning brown.

5 Sprinkle the fruit with the icing sugar and scatter with mint leaves just before serving, if using. Add an extra splash of liqueur, if you wish.

Cook's Tip
If you want to omit the alcohol, use a pure juice substitute such as grape, mango or apricot.

Bombes Energy 715Kcal/2975kJ; Protein 10.6g; Carbohydrate 59.6g, of which sugars 55.1g; Fat 49.7g, of which saturates 29.7g; Cholesterol 21mg; Calcium 269mg; Fibre 0.2g; Sodium 216mg.
Summer Berries Energy 219Kcal/919kJ; Protein 3.9g; Carbohydrate 29.7g, of which sugars 29.7g; Fat 5.6g, of which saturates 1.6g; Cholesterol 202mg; Calcium 50mg; Fibre 1.3g; Sodium 20mg.

Hot Mocha Rum Soufflés

These light-as-air individual soufflés, flavoured with cocoa and coffee, are ideal for serving after a fairly substantial main course.

Serves 6
25g/1oz/2 tbsp unsalted (sweet) butter, melted
65g/2½oz/9 tbsp cocoa powder (unsweetened)
75g/3oz/6 tbsp caster (superfine) sugar
60ml/4 tbsp made-up strong black coffee
30ml/2 tbsp dark rum
6 egg whites
icing (confectioners') sugar, for dusting

1 Preheat the oven to 190°C/375°F/Gas 5. Grease six 250ml/ 8fl oz/1 cup soufflé dishes with melted butter.

2 Mix 15ml/1 tbsp of the cocoa with 15ml/1 tbsp of the caster sugar in a bowl. Sprinkle the mixture into each of the dishes in turn, rotating them so that they are evenly coated.

3 Mix the remaining cocoa with the coffee and rum in a medium bowl.

4 Whisk the egg whites in a clean, grease-free bowl until they form firm peaks. Whisk in the remaining sugar. Stir a generous spoonful of the egg whites into the cocoa mixture to lighten it, then fold in the remaining whites.

5 Spoon the mixture into the prepared dishes, smoothing the tops. Place on a hot baking sheet, and bake for 12–15 minutes or until well risen. Serve immediately, dusted with icing sugar.

> **Cook's Tip**
> *You can use either a hand whisk or an electric version to beat the egg whites, but take care not to overbeat with the electric beaters. The whites should stand in soft peaks, with the tips gently flopping over. Overbeaten eggs will look dry.*

Chocolate & Orange Soufflé

The base in this hot soufflé is an easy-to-make semolina mixture, rather than the thick white sauce that many soufflés call for.

Serves 4
butter, for greasing
600ml/1 pint/2½ cups milk
50g/2oz/generous ⅓ cup semolina
50g/2oz/scant ¼ cup soft light brown sugar
grated rind of 1 orange
90ml/6 tbsp fresh orange juice
3 eggs, separated
75g/3oz plain (semisweet) chocolate, grated
icing (confectioners') sugar, for sprinkling
single (light) cream, to serve

1 Preheat the oven to 200°C/400°F/Gas 6. Butter a shallow 1.75 litre/3 pint/7½ cup ovenproof dish.

2 Pour the milk into a heavy pan, sprinkle over the semolina and sugar, then heat, stirring the mixture constantly, until boiling and thickened.

3 Remove the pan from the heat, beat in the orange rind and juice, egg yolks and all but 15ml/1 tbsp of the grated chocolate.

4 Whisk the egg whites until stiff, then lightly fold one-third into the semolina mixture. Fold in another third, followed by the remaining egg white. Spoon into the buttered dish and bake for about 30 minutes, until just set in the centre.

5 Sprinkle the soufflé with the reserved grated chocolate and the icing sugar, then serve immediately, with the cream handed around separately.

> **Variation**
> *For a sophisticated touch, replace 30ml/2 tbsp of the orange juice with the same amount of orange-flavoured liqueur, such as Cointreau or Grand Marnier.*

Rum Soufflés Energy 148Kcal/619kJ; Protein 5g; Carbohydrate 14.3g, of which sugars 13.1g; Fat 5.8g, of which saturates 3.6g; Cholesterol 9mg; Calcium 23mg; Fibre 1.3g; Sodium 190mg. **Choc. & Orange Soufflé** Energy 321Kcal/1353kJ; Protein 12.2g; Carbohydrate 43.7g, of which sugars 33.8g; Fat 12.2g, of which saturates 5.9g; Cholesterol 153mg; Calcium 219mg; Fibre 0.8g; Sodium 123mg.

Hot Chocolate Soufflés

These rich, individual chocolate soufflés have the merest hint of orange in them, and are divine with the white chocolate sauce poured into the middle.

Serves 6
butter, for greasing
45ml/3 tbsp caster (superfine) sugar, plus extra for dusting
175g/6oz plain (semisweet) chocolate, chopped
150g/5oz/10 tbsp unsalted

(sweet) butter, cut into small pieces
4 large eggs, separated
30ml/2 tbsp orange liqueur (optional)
1.5ml/¼ tsp cream of tartar
icing sugar, for dusting

For the chocolate sauce
75g/3oz white chocolate, chopped
90ml/6 tbsp whipping cream
15–30ml/1–2 tbsp orange liqueur
grated rind of ½ orange

1 Generously butter six 150ml/¼ pint/⅔ cup ramekins. Sprinkle each with a little caster sugar and tap out any excess. Place the ramekins on a baking sheet.

2 Melt the chocolate and butter in a bowl placed over a pan of simmering water, stirring constantly. Remove from the heat and cool slightly, then beat in the egg yolks and orange liqueur, if using. Set aside, stirring occasionally.

3 Preheat the oven to 220°C/425°F/Gas 7. In a large, grease-free bowl, whisk the egg whites slowly until frothy. Add the cream of tartar, increase the speed and whisk until the whites form soft peaks. Gradually sprinkle over the caster sugar, 15ml/ 1 tbsp at a time, whisking until the whites become stiff and glossy.

4 Stir a third of the whites into the cooled chocolate mixture to lighten it, then pour the mixture over the remaining whites.

5 Gently fold the sauce into the whites, cutting down to the bottom, then along the sides and up to the top in a semicircular motion until the chocolate mixture and egg whites are just combined; don't worry about a few white streaks. Spoon the combined mixture into the prepared dishes.

6 Make the white chocolate sauce. Put the chopped white chocolate and the cream into a small pan. Place over a very low heat and warm, stirring constantly, until melted and smooth. Remove from the heat and stir in the liqueur and orange rind, then pour into a serving jug (pitcher) and keep warm.

7 Bake the soufflés in the preheated oven for 10–12 minutes until risen and set, but still slightly wobbly in the centre. Dust with icing sugar and serve immediately with the warm sauce.

> **Cook's Tip**
> These soufflés are ideal for serving at a dinner party because they can be prepared in advance, ready for baking at the last minute. Follow steps 1–5 above, then tightly cover the uncooked soufflés with clear film (plastic wrap). Set aside in a cool, but not cold, place until ready to cook.

Hot Blackberry & Apple Soufflés

The deliciously tart flavours of blackberry and apple complement each other perfectly to make a surprisingly low-fat dessert.

Serves 6
butter, for greasing
150g/5oz/¾ cup caster (superfine) sugar, plus extra for dusting

350g/12oz/3 cups fresh blackberries
1 large cooking apple, peeled and finely diced
grated rind and juice of 1 orange
3 egg whites
icing (confectioners') sugar, for dusting

1 Preheat the oven to 200°C/400°F/Gas 6. Generously grease six 150ml/¼ pint/⅔ cup individual soufflé dishes with butter and dust with sugar, shaking out the excess sugar.

2 Put a baking sheet in the oven to heat. Cook the blackberries, diced apple and orange rind and juice in a pan for 10 minutes or until the apple has pulped down well. Press through a sieve (strainer) into a bowl. Stir in 50g/2oz/¼ cup of the sugar. Cool.

3 Put a spoonful of the fruit purée into each prepared dish and smooth the surface. Set the dishes aside.

4 Whisk the egg whites in a large grease-free bowl until they form stiff peaks. Very gradually whisk in the remaining sugar to make a stiff, glossy meringue mixture. Fold in the remaining fruit purée and spoon into the prepared dishes. Level the tops.

5 Place the dishes on the hot baking sheet and bake for 10–15 minutes until the soufflés have risen well and are lightly browned. Dust the tops with icing sugar and serve immediately.

> **Cook's Tip**
> Run a table knife around the inside edge of the soufflé dishes before baking to help the soufflés rise evenly without sticking to the rim of the dish.

Blackberry & Apple Soufflés Energy 123Kcal/522kJ; Protein 2.1g; Carbohydrate 30.1g, of which sugars 30.1g; Fat 0.1g, of which saturates 0g; Cholesterol 0mg; Calcium 38mg; Fibre 2g; Sodium 33mg.
Chocolate Soufflés Energy 543Kcal/2257kJ; Protein 7.1g; Carbohydrate 35g, of which sugars 34.8g; Fat 42.3g, of which saturates 25g; Cholesterol 198mg; Calcium 80mg; Fibre 0.7g; Sodium 218mg.

Amaretto Soufflé

A mouthwatering soufflé with more than a hint of Amaretto liqueur.

Serves 6

butter, for greasing
90g/3½oz/½ cup caster (superfine) sugar
6 amaretti, coarsely crushed, plus extra for dusting

90ml/6 tbsp Amaretto liqueur
4 eggs, separated, plus 1 egg white
30ml/2 tbsp plain (all-purpose) flour
250ml/8fl oz/1 cup milk
pinch of cream of tartar
icing (confectioners') sugar, for dusting

1 Preheat the oven to 200°C/400°F/Gas 6. Butter a 1.5 litre/2½ pint/6¼ cup soufflé dish and sprinkle it with a little sugar.

2 Put the amaretti in a bowl. Sprinkle them with 30ml/2 tbsp of the Amaretto liqueur and set aside. In another bowl, carefully mix together the 4 egg yolks, 30ml/2 tbsp of the sugar and all of the flour.

3 Heat the milk just to the boil in a heavy pan. Gradually add the hot milk to the egg mixture, stirring. Pour the mixture back into the pan. Set over a low heat and simmer gently for 3–4 minutes or until thickened, stirring occasionally. Add the remaining Amaretto liqueur. Remove from the heat.

4 In a clean, grease-free bowl, whisk the 5 egg whites until they will hold soft peaks. Add the cream of tartar as soon as the whites are frothy. Add the remaining sugar and continue whisking until stiff.

5 Add about one-quarter of the whites to the liqueur mixture and stir in. Add the remaining whites and fold in gently. Spoon half of the mixture into the prepared soufflé dish. Cover with a layer of the moistened amaretti, then spoon the remaining soufflé mixture on top.

6 Bake for 20 minutes or until the soufflé is risen and lightly browned. Sprinkle with sifted icing sugar and serve immediately.

Pears in Chocolate Fudge Blankets

Warm poached pears coated in a rich chocolate fudge sauce – who could resist?

Serves 6

6 ripe eating pears
30ml/2 tbsp fresh lemon juice
75g/3oz/6 tbsp caster (superfine) sugar
300ml/½ pint/1¼ cups water
1 cinnamon stick

For the sauce
200ml/7fl oz/scant 1 cup double (heavy) cream
150g/5oz/scant 1 cup light muscovado (brown) sugar
25g/1oz/2 tbsp unsalted (sweet) butter
60ml/4 tbsp golden (light corn) syrup
120ml/4fl oz/½ cup milk
200g/7oz plain (semisweet) chocolate, broken into squares

1 Peel the pears thinly, leaving the stalks on. Scoop out the cores from the base. Brush the cut surfaces with lemon juice to prevent browning.

2 Place the sugar and water in a large pan. Heat gently until the sugar dissolves. Add the pears and cinnamon stick with any remaining lemon juice, and, if necessary, a little more water, so that the pears are almost covered.

3 Bring to the boil, then lower the heat, cover the pan and simmer the pears gently for 15–20 minutes.

4 Meanwhile, make the sauce. Place the cream, sugar, butter, golden syrup and milk in a heavy pan. Heat gently until the sugar has dissolved and the butter and syrup have melted, then bring to the boil. Boil, stirring constantly, for about 5 minutes or until thick and smooth.

5 Remove the pan from the heat and stir in the chocolate, a few squares at a time, stirring until it has all melted.

6 Using a slotted spoon, transfer the poached pears to a dish. Keep hot. Boil the syrup rapidly to reduce to 45–60ml/3–4 tbsp. Remove the cinnamon stick and gently stir the syrup into the chocolate sauce. Serve the pears with the sauce spooned over.

Amaretto Soufflé Energy 222Kcal/936kJ; Protein 7.1g; Carbohydrate 33g, of which sugars 25.6g; Fat 5.6g, of which saturates 2g; Cholesterol 129mg; Calcium 96mg; Fibre 0.3g; Sodium 105mg.
Fudge Blankets Energy 613Kcal/2570kJ; Protein 3.6g; Carbohydrate 84.8g, of which sugars 84.5g; Fat 31.2g, of which saturates 19.1g; Cholesterol 58mg; Calcium 90mg; Fibre 4.1g; Sodium 77mg.

Citrus & Caramel Custards

These are wonderfully smooth and delicious custards – delicately scented and enhanced with aromatic cinnamon and tangy citrus flavours.

Serves 4
450ml/¾ pint/scant 2 cups milk
150ml/¼ pint/⅔ cup single (light) cream

1 cinnamon stick, broken in half
thinly pared rind of ½ lemon
thinly pared rind of ½ orange
4 egg yolks
5ml/1 tsp cornflour (cornstarch)
40g/1½oz/3 tbsp caster (superfine) sugar
grated rind of ½ lemon
grated rind of ½ orange
icing (confectioners') sugar, to dust

1 Place the milk and cream in a heavy pan. Add the cinnamon stick halves and the strips of pared lemon and orange rind.

2 Bring this milk to the boil, then reduce the heat and simmer for 10 minutes. Preheat the oven to 160°C/325°F/Gas 3.

3 Whisk the egg yolks, cornflour and sugar together. Remove the citrus fruit rinds and cinnamon from the hot milk and cream and discard. Whisk the hot milk and cream into the egg yolk mixture.

4 Add the grated citrus rind to the custard mixture and stir through. Pour into four individual dishes, each measuring 13cm/5in in diameter.

5 Place in a roasting pan and pour warm water into the pan to reach three-quarters of the way up the sides.

6 Bake for about 25 minutes, or until the caramel custards are just set. Remove all of the dishes from the pan of water and set them aside to cool thoroughly. Once cool, chill the custards in the refrigerator.

7 Preheat the grill (broiler) to high. Sprinkle the custards liberally with icing sugar and place under the grill until the tops turn golden brown and caramelize.

Coconut Pancakes

These light and sweet pancakes are often served in the streets of Bangkok and they make a delightful dessert.

Makes 8
75g/3oz/⅔ cup plain (all-purpose) flour, sifted
50g/2oz/¼ cup rice flour

40g/1½oz caster (superfine) sugar
50g/2oz/⅔ cup desiccated (dry unsweetened shredded) coconut
1 egg
275ml/9fl oz/generous 1 cup coconut milk
vegetable oil, for frying
lime wedges and maple syrup, to serve

1 Place the plain flour, rice flour, sugar and coconut in a bowl, stir to mix and then make a small well in the centre. Break the egg into the well and pour in the coconut milk.

2 With a whisk or fork, beat the egg into the coconut milk and then gradually incorporate the surrounding dry ingredients, whisking constantly until the mixture forms a batter. The mixture will not be entirely smooth, because of the coconut, but there shouldn't be any large lumps.

3 Heat a little oil in a 13cm/5in non-stick frying pan. Pour in about 45ml/3 tbsp of the mixture and quickly spread to a thin layer with the back of a spoon. Cook over a high heat for about 30–60 seconds, until bubbles appear on the surface of the pancake, then turn it over with a spatula and cook the other side until golden.

4 Slide the pancake on to a plate and keep warm in a very low oven. Make more pancakes in the same way. Serve warm with lime wedges for squeezing and maple syrup for drizzling.

Cook's Tip
Although maple syrup is not a typical Thai ingredient, it is an international favourite for serving with pancakes and tastes very good with these ones. Buy the pure syrup for the best flavour.

Custards Energy 229Kcal/958kJ; Protein 8g; Carbohydrate 17.7g, of which sugars 16.6g; Fat 14.6g, of which saturates 7.3g; Cholesterol 229mg; Calcium 197mg; Fibre 0g; Sodium 70mg.
Pancakes Energy 136Kcal/572kJ; Protein 2.6g; Carbohydrate 21.3g, of which sugars 8.1g; Fat 4.9g, of which saturates 3.6g; Cholesterol 24mg; Calcium 33mg; Fibre 1.3g; Sodium 49mg.

Chocolate & Orange Scotch Pancakes

Fabulous mini pancakes in a rich orange liqueur sauce.

Serves 4

115g/4oz/1 cup self-raising (self-rising) flour
30ml/2 tbsp cocoa powder (unsweetened)
2 eggs
50g/2oz plain (semisweet) chocolate, broken into squares
200ml/7fl oz/scant 1 cup milk
finely grated rind of 1 orange
30ml/2 tbsp orange juice
butter or oil, for frying
60ml/4 tbsp chocolate curls, to decorate

For the sauce

2 large oranges
25g/1oz/2 tbsp unsalted (sweet) butter
40g/1½oz/3 tbsp light muscovado (brown) sugar
250ml/8fl oz/1 cup crème fraîche
30ml/2 tbsp orange liqueur

1 Sift the flour and cocoa into a bowl and make a well in the centre. Add the eggs and beat well, gradually incorporating the surrounding dry ingredients to make a smooth batter.

2 Mix the chocolate and milk in a heavy pan. Heat gently until the chocolate has melted, then beat into the batter until smooth and bubbly. Stir in the grated orange rind and juice.

3 Heat a large heavy frying pan or griddle. Grease with a little butter or oil. Drop large spoonfuls of batter on to the hot surface. Cook over a moderate heat. When the pancakes are lightly browned underneath and bubbling on top, flip them over to cook the other side. Slide on to a plate and keep hot, then make more in the same way.

4 Make the sauce. Grate the rind of 1 of the oranges into a bowl and set aside. Peel both oranges, taking care to remove all the pith, then slice the flesh fairly thinly. Heat the butter and sugar in a wide, shallow pan over a low heat, stirring until the sugar dissolves. Stir in the crème fraîche and heat gently.

5 Add the pancakes and orange slices to the sauce, heat gently for 1–2 minutes, then spoon on the liqueur. Sprinkle with the reserved orange rind. Scatter over chocolate curls and serve.

Chocolate Crêpes with Plums & Port

The crêpes, filling and sauce can be made in advance and assembled at the last minute.

Serves 6

50g/2oz plain (semisweet) chocolate, broken into squares
200ml/7fl oz/scant 1 cup milk
120ml/4fl oz/½ cup single (light) cream
30ml/2 tbsp cocoa powder (unsweetened)
115g/4oz/1 cup plain (all-purpose) flour
2 eggs

For the filling

500g/1¼lb red or golden plums
50g/2oz/¼ cup caster (superfine) sugar
30ml/2 tbsp water
30ml/2 tbsp port
oil, for frying
175g/6oz/¾ cup crème fraîche

For the sauce

150g/5oz plain (semisweet) chocolate, broken into squares
175ml/6fl oz/¾ cup double (heavy) cream
30ml/2 tbsp port

1 Place the chocolate and milk in a heavy pan. Heat gently until the chocolate dissolves. Pour into a blender or food processor and add the cream, cocoa, flour and eggs. Process until smooth. Turn into a jug (pitcher) and chill for 30 minutes.

2 Meanwhile, make the filling. Halve and stone (pit) the plums. Place in a pan with the sugar and water. Bring to the boil, then lower the heat, cover and simmer for about 10 minutes or until the plums are tender. Stir in the port and simmer for a further 30 seconds. Remove from the heat and keep warm.

3 Have ready a sheet of baking parchment. Heat a crêpe pan, grease lightly with a little oil, then pour in just enough batter to cover the base of the pan, swirling to coat it evenly. Cook until the crêpe has set, then flip it over to cook the other side. Slide on to the paper, then cook 9–11 more crêpes in the same way.

4 Make the sauce. Put the chocolate and cream in a pan. Heat gently, stirring until smooth. Add the port and stir for 1 minute.

5 Divide the plums between the crêpes, add a dollop of crème fraîche to each and roll up. Serve with the sauce spooned over.

Pancakes Energy 752Kcal/3131kJ; Protein 12.1g; Carbohydrate 58.1g, of which sugars 35.5g; Fat 53.2g, of which saturates 27g; Cholesterol 185mg; Calcium 282mg; Fibre 3.9g; Sodium 304mg.
Crêpes Energy 867Kcal/3604kJ; Protein 10.6g; Carbohydrate 57.4g, of which sugars 41.7g; Fat 67g, of which saturates 36.7g; Cholesterol 184mg; Calcium 175mg; Fibre 3.4g; Sodium 115mg.

Steamed Chocolate & Fruit Puddings

Some things always turn out well, just like these wonderful little puddings. Dark, fluffy chocolate sponge with tangy cranberries and apple is served with a honeyed chocolate syrup.

Serves 4
butter or oil, for greasing
115g/4oz/½ cup muscovado
  (molasses) sugar
1 eating apple, peeled and cored
75g/3oz/¾ cup cranberries,
  thawed if frozen
115g/4oz/½ cup soft margarine
2 eggs
75g/3oz/⅔ cup plain
  (all-purpose) flour
2.5ml/½ tsp baking powder
45ml/3 tbsp cocoa powder
  (unsweetened)

For the chocolate syrup
115g/4oz plain (semisweet)
  chocolate, broken into squares
30ml/2 tbsp clear honey
15ml/1 tbsp unsalted (sweet)
  butter
2.5ml/½ tsp vanilla extract

1 Prepare a steamer or half fill a pan with water and bring it to the boil. Grease four individual heatproof bowls and sprinkle each one with a little of the muscovado sugar to coat all over.

2 Dice the apple into a bowl. Add the cranberries and mix well. Divide the mixture equally among the prepared bowls.

3 Put the remaining sugar in a mixing bowl. Add the margarine, eggs, flour, baking powder and cocoa. Beat well until smooth.

4 Spoon the mixture into the bowls, on top of the fruit, and cover each with a double thickness of foil. Steam for about 45 minutes, topping up the boiling water as required, until the puddings are well risen and firm.

5 Make the syrup. Mix together the chocolate, honey, butter and vanilla in a small pan. Heat gently, stirring, until smooth.

6 Run a knife around the edge of each pudding to loosen it, then turn out on to individual plates. Serve immediately, with the chocolate syrup poured over the top.

Chocolate Chip & Banana Pudding

Hot and steamy, this superb light pudding tastes extra special when served with ready-made fresh chocolate sauce or custard.

Serves 4
200g/7oz/1¾ cups self-raising
  (self-rising) flour
75g/3oz/6 tbsp unsalted (sweet)
  butter or margarine
2 ripe bananas
75g/3oz/6 tbsp caster
  (superfine) sugar
60ml/4 tbsp milk
1 egg, beaten
60ml/4 tbsp plain (bittersweet)
  chocolate chips or chopped
  chocolate
whipped cream, to serve

1 Prepare a steamer or half fill a pan with water and bring to the boil. Grease a 1 litre/1¾ pint/4 cup ovenproof bowl.

2 Sift the flour into a mixing bowl and rub in the butter or margarine until the mixture resembles breadcrumbs. Mash the bananas in a bowl. Stir them into the creamed mixture, with the caster sugar.

3 Whisk the milk with the egg in a bowl, then beat into the pudding mixture. Stir in the chocolate.

4 Spoon the mixture into the prepared bowl, cover closely with a double thickness of foil, and steam for 2 hours, topping up the water as required during cooking.

5 Run a knife around the top edge of the pudding to loosen it, then turn it out on to a warm serving dish. Serve hot, with a spoonful of whipped cream.

Cook's Tip
If you have a food processor, make a quick-mix version by processing all the ingredients, except the chocolate, until smooth. Then stir in the chocolate, spoon into the prepared bowl and finish as described in the recipe.

Fruit Puddings Energy 672Kcal/2811kJ; Protein 8.7g; Carbohydrate 73.1g, of which sugars 57.3g; Fat 40.4g, of which saturates 13.9g; Cholesterol 105mg; Calcium 84mg; Fibre 3.2g; Sodium 366mg.
Banana Pudding Energy 528Kcal/2220kJ; Protein 8.1g; Carbohydrate 79.3g, of which sugars 40.9g; Fat 22g, of which saturates 13g; Cholesterol 89mg; Calcium 222mg; Fibre 2.5g; Sodium 320mg.

Maple & Pecan Croissant Pudding

This variation of the classic English bread and butter pudding uses rich, flaky croissants, topped with a delicious mixture of fruit and nuts. Custard flavoured with maple syrup completes this mouthwatering dessert.

Serves 4

75g/3oz/scant ½ cup sultanas (golden raisins)
45ml/3 tbsp brandy
4 large croissants
50g/2oz/¼ cup butter or margarine, plus extra for greasing
40g/1½oz/⅓ cup pecan nuts, roughly chopped
3 eggs, lightly beaten
300ml/½ pint/1¼ cups milk
150ml/¼ pint/⅔ cup single (light) cream
120ml/4fl oz/½ cup maple syrup
25g/1oz/2 tbsp demerara (raw) sugar
maple syrup and pouring (half-and-half) cream, to serve

1 Lightly grease the base and sides of a small, shallow ovenproof dish. Place the sultanas and brandy in a small pan and heat gently, until warm. Leave to stand for 1 hour.

2 Cut the croissants into thick slices and spread with butter on one side. Arrange the slices, buttered side uppermost and slightly overlapping, in the greased dish. Sprinkle the brandy-soaked sultanas and the pecan nuts evenly over the croissant slices.

3 In a large bowl, beat the eggs and milk together, then gradually beat in the single cream and maple syrup. Pour the egg custard through a sieve (strainer), over the croissants, fruit and nuts in the dish. Leave the pudding to stand for 30 minutes so that some of the custard is absorbed by the croissants. Meanwhile, preheat the oven to 180°F/350°C/Gas 4.

4 Sprinkle the demerara sugar evenly over the top, then cover the dish with foil. Bake the pudding for 30 minutes, then remove the foil and continue to cook for about 20 minutes, or until the custard is set and the top is golden brown.

5 Leave the pudding to cool for about 15 minutes before serving warm with extra maple syrup and pouring cream.

Fresh Currant Bread & Butter Pudding

Fresh mixed currants add a tart touch to this scrumptious hot pudding.

Serves 6

8 medium-thick slices day-old bread, crusts removed
50g/2oz/¼ cup butter, softened
115g/4oz/1 cup redcurrants
115g/4oz/1 cup blackcurrants
4 eggs, beaten
75g/3oz/6 tbsp caster (superfine) sugar
475ml/16fl oz/2 cups creamy milk
5ml/1 tsp pure vanilla extract
freshly grated nutmeg
30ml/2 tbsp demerara (raw) sugar
single (light) cream, to serve

1 Preheat the oven to 160°C/325°F/Gas 3. Generously butter a 1.2 litre/2 pint/5 cup oval baking dish.

2 Spread the slices of bread generously with the butter, then cut them in half diagonally. Layer the slices in the dish, buttered side up, sprinkling the currants between the layers.

3 Beat the eggs and caster sugar lightly together in a large mixing bowl, then gradually whisk in the milk, vanilla extract and a large pinch of freshly grated nutmeg. Pour the milk mixture over the bread, pushing the slices down. Sprinkle the demerara sugar and a little nutmeg over the top.

4 Place the dish in a roasting pan and then add hot water so that the water reaches halfway up the sides of the dish. Bake for 40 minutes, then increase the oven temperature to 180°C/350°F/Gas 4 and bake for 20–25 minutes until golden. Serve with single cream.

Variation
A mixture of blueberries and raspberries would work very successfully instead of the currants.

Croissant Pudding Energy 738Kcal/3088kJ; Protein 15.1g; Carbohydrate 74.2g, of which sugars 51.3g; Fat 45.6g, of which saturates 19.5g; Cholesterol 226mg; Calcium 218mg; Fibre 1.8g; Sodium 508mg.
Bread & But. Pudding Energy 328Kcal/1377kJ; Protein 10.3g; Carbohydrate 42.2g, of which sugars 25.4g; Fat 14.3g, of which saturates 7.4g; Cholesterol 156mg; Calcium 186mg; Fibre 1.9g; Sodium 321mg.

Moroccan Rice Pudding

A simple and delicious alternative to a traditional British rice pudding. The rice is cooked in almond-flavoured milk and delicately highlighted with cinnamon and orange flower water.

Serves 6
25g/1oz/¼ cup almonds, chopped
450g/1lb/2¼ cups pudding (short grain) rice
25g/1oz/¼ cup icing (confectioners') sugar
1 cinnamon stick
50g/2oz/¼ cup butter or margarine
1.5ml/¼ tsp almond extract
175ml/6fl oz/¾ cup milk
175ml/6fl oz/¾ cup single (light) cream
30ml/2 tbsp orange flower water
toasted flaked (sliced) almonds and ground cinnamon, to decorate

1 Put the almonds in a food processor or blender with 60ml/4 tbsp very hot water. Process until the almonds are finely chopped, then push through a sieve (strainer) into a bowl. Return the almond mixture to the food processor or blender, add a further 60ml/4 tbsp very hot water, and process again. Push the almond mixture through the sieve into a pan.

2 Add 300ml/½ pint/1¼ cups water and bring the mixture to the boil. Add the rice, icing sugar, cinnamon stick, half the butter, the almond extract, half the milk and half the cream.

3 Bring to the boil, then simmer, covered, for about 30 minutes, adding more milk and cream as the rice mixture thickens. Continue to cook the rice, stirring and adding the remaining milk and cream, until the pudding becomes thick and creamy.

4 Stir in the orange flower water, then taste the rice pudding for sweetness, adding a little extra sugar, if necessary.

5 Pour the rice pudding into a serving bowl and sprinkle with the toasted flaked almonds. Dot with the remaining butter and dust with a little ground cinnamon. Serve the pudding hot.

Baked Rice Pudding, Thai-style

Black glutinous rice, also known as black sticky rice, has long dark grains and a nutty taste reminiscent of wild rice. This baked pudding has a distinct character and flavour all of its own, as well as an intriguing appearance.

Serves 4–6
175g/6oz/1 cup white or black glutinous rice
30ml/2 tbsp soft light brown sugar
475ml/16fl oz/2 cups coconut milk
250ml/8fl oz/1 cup water
3 eggs
30ml/2 tbsp granulated sugar

1 Combine the glutinous rice and brown sugar in a pan. Pour in half the coconut milk and the water.

2 Bring to the boil, reduce the heat to low and simmer, stirring occasionally, for 15–20 minutes, or until the rice has absorbed most of the liquid. Preheat the oven to 150°C/300°F/Gas 2.

3 Spoon the rice mixture into a single large ovenproof dish or divide it among individual ramekins. Beat the eggs with the remaining coconut milk and sugar in a bowl.

4 Strain the egg mixture into a jug (pitcher), then pour it evenly over the par-cooked rice in the dish or ramekins.

5 Place the dish or ramekins in a roasting pan. Carefully pour in enough hot water to come halfway up the sides of the dish or ramekins.

6 Cover with foil and bake for about 35–60 minutes, or until the custard has set. Serve warm.

Cook's Tip
Throughout South-east Asia, black glutinous rice is usually used to make sweet dishes, while its white counterpart is more often used in savoury recipes.

Exotic Tapioca Pudding

This pudding, made from large pearl tapioca and coconut milk and served warm, is much lighter than the traditional Western-style version. You can adjust the sweetness to your taste. Serve with lychees or the smaller, similar-tasting longans – also known as "dragon's eyes".

Serves 4

115g/4oz/⅔ cup tapioca
475ml/16fl oz/2 cups water
175g/6oz/¾ cup granulated
    sugar
pinch of salt
250ml/8fl oz/1 cup coconut milk
250g/9oz prepared tropical fruits
finely shredded lime rind and
    shaved fresh coconut (optional),
    to decorate

1 Put the tapioca in a bowl and pour over enough warm water to cover completely. Leave to soak for 1 hour so the grains swell. Drain well.

2 Pour the measured water in a large pan and bring to the boil over a medium heat. Add the sugar and salt and stir until completely dissolved.

3 Add the tapioca and coconut milk, reduce the heat to low and simmer gently for 10 minutes, or until the tapioca becomes tender and transparent.

4 Spoon into one large or four individual bowls and serve warm with the tropical fruits. Decorate with the lime rind and coconut shavings, if using.

Cook's Tip
• *Tapioca pearls are a product of cassava, which is a tropical root plant, originating in America. Cassava flour is processed to form the pearls. In the past, tapioca milk pudding was a popular British dessert.*
• *For a tropical fruit accompaniment, arrange sliced and peeled pineapple, ripe mango and papaya on a platter with chunks of oranges for added juiciness. Sprinkle with finely grated lime rind.*

Fragrant Rice with Dates

The rice puddings that are popular all over Morocco are served liberally sprinkled with either nuts and honey or wrapped in pastry. This is a low-fat version.

Serves 4

75g/3oz/½ cup pudding (short
    grain) rice
about 900ml/1½ pints/3¾ cups
    skimmed milk
30ml/2 tbsp ground rice
50g/2oz/¼ cup caster (superfine)
    sugar
15g/½oz/2 tbsp ground almonds
5ml/1 tsp vanilla extract
2.5ml/½ tsp almond extract
a little orange flower water
    (optional)
30ml/2 tbsp chopped dates
30ml/2 tbsp unsalted pistachio
    nuts, finely chopped

1 Place the rice in a pan with 750ml/1¼ pints/3 cups of the milk and gradually heat until simmering. Cook, uncovered, over a very low heat for 30–40 minutes, until the rice is completely tender, stirring frequently.

2 Blend the ground rice with the remaining milk and add to the pan, stirring. Slowly bring back to the boil and continue to cook for 1 minute.

3 Stir in the sugar, ground almonds, vanilla and almond extracts and orange flower water, if using. Cook, stirring frequently, until the pudding is thick and creamy.

4 Pour into serving bowls and sprinkle with the chopped dates and pistachios. Allow to cool slightly before serving.

Cook's Tip
• *Orange flower water, made from the flowers of the bitter orange, is a traditional ingredient of the Middle East, where it is used to add delicate fragrance to all manner of desserts.*
• *Chopped ready-to-eat dried apricots and toasted flaked (sliced) almonds also make a good topping for the dish, complementing the flavours of the rice.*

Tapioca Pudding Energy 325Kcal/1388kJ; Protein 1g; Carbohydrate 84.9g, of which sugars 57.4g; Fat 0.4g, of which saturates 0.2g; Cholesterol 0mg; Calcium 51mg; Fibre 1.8g; Sodium 74mg.
Fragrant Rice Energy 302Kcal/1272kJ; Protein 11.2g; Carbohydrate 46.7g, of which sugars 26.4g; Fat 8.4g, of which saturates 3g; Cholesterol 13mg; Calcium 292mg; Fibre 0.8g; Sodium 139mg.

Baked Apples with Red Wine

These mouthwatering baked apples are packed with goodness. Flavoured with a delicious filling of dried fruit soaked in spiced red wine, they are certainly worthy of a dinner party.

Serves 6
65g/2½oz/scant ½ cup sultanas (golden raisins)
350ml/12fl oz/1½ cups red wine
pinch of grated nutmeg
pinch of ground cinnamon
50g/2oz/¼ cup granulated sugar
pinch of grated lemon rind
35ml/7 tsp low-fat spread
6 even-size cooking apples

1 Put the sultanas in a small bowl and pour over the wine. Stir in the grated nutmeg, ground cinnamon, sugar and lemon rind. Cover and leave to stand for about 1 hour.

2 Preheat the oven to 190°C/375°F/Gas 5. Use a little of the low-fat spread to grease a baking dish. Using an apple corer, remove the core of each apple, without cutting right through to the bottom.

3 Divide the sultana mixture among the apples, carefully packing it into the hollows. Spoon in a little extra spiced wine. Arrange the apples in the prepared baking dish.

4 Pour the remaining wine around the apples. Top the filling in each apple with 5ml/1 tsp of the remaining spread. Bake for 40–50 minutes, or until the apples are soft but not mushy. Serve hot or at room temperature.

Cook's Tips
• If you want to reduce the fat content to almost nothing, do not top each apple with the spread. The fat does add a certain richness to the dish, but is not completely necessary as the wine provides enough moisture in which to cook the apples.
• Make sure that the apples do not overcook, as this will ruin the look and texture of the dish. Test with a knife.

Fruity Bread Pudding

A delicious family favourite from grandmother's kitchen, with a lighter, healthier touch for today.

Serves 4
75g/3oz/½ cup mixed dried fruit
150ml/¼ pint/⅔ cup unsweetened apple juice
115g/4oz/3–4 slices day-old brown or white bread, cubed
5ml/1 tsp mixed spice (apple pie spice)
1 large banana, sliced
150ml/¼ pint/⅔ cup skimmed milk
15ml/1 tbsp demerara (raw) sugar
fat-free natural (plain) yogurt, to serve (optional)

1 Preheat the oven to 200°C/400°F/Gas 6. Place the dried fruit in a small pan with the apple juice and bring to the boil.

2 Remove the pan from the heat and stir in the bread cubes, spice and banana. Spoon the mixture into a shallow 1.2 litre/2 pint/5 cup ovenproof dish and pour over the milk.

3 Sprinkle the top with demerara sugar and bake in the oven for 25–30 minutes, until firm and golden brown. Serve hot or cold, with yogurt, if you like.

Baked Apples in Honey & Lemon

A classic combination of flavours in a healthy, traditional dessert.

Serves 4
4 even-size cooking apples
15ml/1 tbsp clear honey
grated rind and juice of 1 lemon
15ml/1 tbsp low-fat spread
fresh custard, made with skimmed milk, to serve (optional)

1 Preheat the oven to 180°C/350°F/Gas 4. Using an apple corer, remove the cores from the apples, taking care not to go right through the bottoms of the apples.

2 Using a zester or a sharp knife with a narrow pointed blade, cut lines through the apple skin at intervals. Stand the apples in an ovenproof dish.

3 Place the honey in a bowl and mix in the lemon rind and juice and low-fat spread.

4 Spoon the mixture into the apples and cover the dish with foil or a lid. Bake in the oven for 40-45 minutes, or until the apples are tender. Serve with fresh custard made from skimmed milk, if you like.

Variation
You can always add dried fruit, such as chopped apricots or raisins, to the hollowed out core instead of honey — dried fruit adds natural sweetness and ups the fibre and vitamin content.

Apples/Red Wine Energy 149Kcal/627kJ; Protein 0.9g; Carbohydrate 22.3g, of which sugars 22.3g; Fat 2.5g, of which saturates 0.7g; Cholesterol 0mg; Calcium 20mg; Fibre 1.3g; Sodium 46mg.
Bread Pudding Energy 178Kcal/759kJ; Protein 4.4g; Carbohydrate 40.9g, of which sugars 27g; Fat 0.8g, of which saturates 0.1g; Cholesterol 1mg; Calcium 97mg; Fibre 1.1g; Sodium 176mg.
Apples/Honey & Lemon Energy 51Kcal/216kJ; Protein 0.5g; Carbohydrate 9.3g, of which sugars 9.3g; Fat 1.6g, of which saturates 0.4g; Cholesterol 0mg; Calcium 5mg; Fibre 1.2g; Sodium 26mg. .

Sultana & Couscous Puddings

Couscous makes an interesting alternative to rice. In this recipe, it is flavoured with fruit, then steamed in moulds and turned out to make unusual fat-free desserts.

Serves 4
50g/2oz/⅓ cup sultanas (golden raisins)
475ml/16fl oz/2 cups unsweetened apple juice
90g/3½oz/generous 1 cup couscous
2.5ml/½ tsp mixed spice (apple pie spice)
fresh skimmed milk custard, to serve (optional)

1 Lightly grease four 250ml/8fl oz/1 cup heatproof bowls. Place the sultanas and apple juice in a pan.

2 Bring the apple juice to the boil, then lower the heat and simmer the mixture gently for 2–3 minutes, to plump up the fruit. Lift out about half of the fruit and place it in the bottom of the bowls.

3 Add the couscous and mixed spice to the pan and bring the liquid back to the boil, stirring. Cover and leave over a low heat for 8–10 minutes, or until all the liquid has been absorbed.

4 Spoon the couscous into the bowls, level the surfaces, then cover the bowls tightly with foil. Place the bowls in a steamer over boiling water, cover and steam for about 30 minutes. Run a knife around the edges, turn the puddings out carefully and serve straight away, with skimmed milk custard, if you like.

Cook's Tips
• If you prefer, these delicious puddings can easily be cooked in a microwave oven instead of steaming over boiling water. To do this, simply use individual microwave-safe basins or teacups, cover them and then microwave on High for approximately 8–10 minutes.

Baked Peaches with Raspberry Sauce

It's always a good idea to round off a meal on a light and fruity note. Everyone will enjoy these stuffed peaches, which also look very pretty.

Serves 4
30ml/2 tbsp low-fat spread
50g/2oz/¼ cup granulated sugar
1 egg, beaten

25g/1oz/¼ cup ground almonds
6 ripe peaches
glossy leaves and plain or frosted raspberries, to decorate

For the sauce
350g/12oz/2 cups raspberries
15ml/1 tbsp icing (confectioners') sugar

1 Preheat the oven to 180°C/350°F/Gas 4. Beat the low-fat spread and sugar together in a bowl, then beat in the egg and ground almonds.

2 Cut the peaches in half and remove the stones (pits). With a spoon, scrape out some of the flesh from each peach half, slightly enlarging the hollow left by the stone. Save the excess peach flesh for the sauce.

3 Stand the peach halves on a baking sheet, supporting them with crumpled foil to keep them steady. Fill the hollow in each peach half with the almond mixture.

4 Bake in the preheated oven for 30 minutes, or until the almond filling is puffed and golden and the peaches are tender.

5 Meanwhile, make the sauce. Combine the raspberries and icing sugar in a food processor or blender. Add the reserved peach flesh and process until smooth. Press through a sieve (strainer) set over a bowl, to remove the fibres and seeds.

6 Allow the peaches to cool slightly. Spoon the sauce on to each plate and arrange two peach halves on top. Decorate with the leaves and raspberries and serve immediately.

Couscous Puddings Energy 131Kcal/555kJ; Protein 1.8g; Carbohydrate 32g, of which sugars 20.4g; Fat 0.4g, of which saturates 0g; Cholesterol 0mg; Calcium 21mg; Fibre 0.3g; Sodium 5mg.
Baked Peaches Energy 223Kcal/945kJ; Protein 6.1g; Carbohydrate 33.5g, of which sugars 33.3g; Fat 8.3g, of which saturates 1.6g; Cholesterol 48mg; Calcium 64mg; Fibre 4.8g; Sodium 72mg.

Warm Lemon & Syrup Cake

The combination of pears, sticky syrup and lemon makes this a real winner. Drizzle with thin cream for extra luxury.

Serves 8
3 eggs
175g/6oz/¾ cup butter, softened
175g/6oz/¾ cup caster (superfine) sugar
175g/6oz/1½ cups self-raising (self-rising) flour
50g/2oz/½ cup ground almonds
1.5ml/¼ tsp freshly grated nutmeg
50g/2oz/5 tbsp candied lemon peel, finely chopped
grated rind of 1 lemon
30ml/2 tbsp lemon juice
poached pears, to serve

For the syrup
175g/6oz/¾ cup caster (superfine) sugar
juice of 3 lemons
75ml/3 tbsp water

1 Preheat the oven to 180°C/350°F/Gas 4. Grease and base-line a deep, round 20cm/8in cake tin (pan).

2 Place all the cake ingredients in a large bowl and beat well for 2–3 minutes, until the mixture is light and fluffy.

3 Transfer the mixture to the prepared tin, spread level and bake for 1 hour, or until golden and firm to the touch.

4 Meanwhile, make the syrup. Put the sugar, lemon juice and water in a pan. Heat gently, stirring until the sugar has dissolved, then boil, without stirring, for 1–2 minutes.

5 Turn the cake out on to a plate with a rim. Prick the surface of the cake all over with a fork, then pour over the hot syrup. Leave to soak for about 30 minutes. Serve the cake warm with thin wedges of poached pears.

Cook's Tip
To speed up the preparation, mix the ingredients together in a food processor, but take care not to overbeat.

Spiced Pear & Blueberry Parcels

Baked in foil parcels, the pears and blueberries happily cook in their own juices, making this a low-fat method of turning fruit into a hot dessert.

Serves 4
4 firm, ripe pears
30ml/2 tbsp lemon juice
15ml/1 tbsp low-fat spread, melted
150g/5oz/1¼ cups blueberries
50g/2oz/¼ cup light muscovado (brown) sugar
ground black pepper

1 Prepare a barbecue or preheat the oven to 200°C/400°F/Gas 6. Peel the pears thinly. Cut in half lengthways. Scoop out the core from each half. Brush the pears with lemon juice, to stop them browning.

2 Cut four squares of double-thickness foil, each large enough to wrap a pear, and brush with melted spread. Place two pear halves on each square, cut side upwards. Gather the foil around the pears, to hold them level.

3 Mix the blueberries and sugar together and spoon them on top of the pears. Sprinkle with black pepper. Wrap the foil over and make sure it is properly sealed. Cook for 20–25 minutes on the rack of a fairly hot barbecue or in the preheated oven, until the fruit is tender.

Cook's Tip
To assemble the dessert in advance, place waxed paper inside the parcel, because the acid in the lemon juice may react with the foil and taint the flavour.

Variation
Add a dash of Kirsch just before sealing the parcel, to give a sophisticated flavour to the dessert.

Lemon Cake Energy 488Kcal/2047kJ; Protein 6g; Carbohydrate 66.5g, of which sugars 50.1g; Fat 23.9g, of which saturates 12.3g; Cholesterol 118mg; Calcium 138mg; Fibre 1.4g; Sodium 259mg.
Spiced Parcels Energy 143Kcal/605kJ; Protein 1.1g; Carbohydrate 32.6g, of which sugars 32.6g; Fat 1.8g, of which saturates 0.4g; Cholesterol 0mg; Calcium 41mg; Fibre 4.5g; Sodium 31mg.

Mexican Citrus Rice Pudding

Rice is a versatile, healthy ingredient and in this Mexican recipe it is transformed into a light and attractive dessert, perfect for a family meal.

Serves 4
75g/3oz/½ cup raisins
90g/3½oz/½ cup pudding (short-grain) rice
2.5cm/1in strip of pared lime or lemon rind
250ml/8fl oz/1 cup water
475ml/16fl oz/2 cups skimmed milk
225g/8oz/1 cup granulated sugar
1.5ml/¼ tsp salt
2.5cm/1in cinnamon stick
1 egg yolk, well beaten
15ml/1 tbsp low-fat spread
10ml/2 tsp toasted flaked (sliced) almonds, to decorate
orange segments, to serve

1 Put the raisins into a small bowl. Cover with warm water and set aside to soak.

2 Put the rice into a pan together with the pared lime or lemon rind and water. Bring slowly to the boil, then lower the heat. Cover the pan and simmer gently for about 20 minutes or until all the water has been absorbed.

3 Remove the rind from the rice and discard it. Add the milk, sugar, salt and cinnamon stick. Cook, stirring, over a very low heat until all the milk has been absorbed. Do not cover the pan during cooking.

4 Discard the cinnamon stick. Drain the raisins well. Add the raisins, egg yolk and low-fat spread to the rice, stirring constantly until the spread has been absorbed and the pudding is rich and creamy.

5 Cook the pudding for a few minutes longer. Transfer the rice to a serving dish and allow to cool.

6 Decorate with the toasted flaked almonds and serve with the orange segments.

Sticky Toffee Pudding

Filling and warming, this tasty variation on a classic pudding will soon become a firm family favourite.

Serves 6
115g/4oz/1 cup toasted walnuts, chopped
175g/6oz/¾ cup butter
175g/6oz/scant 1 cup soft brown sugar
60ml/4 tbsp single (light) cream
30ml/2 tbsp freshly squeezed lemon juice
2 eggs, beaten
115g/4oz/1 cup self-raising (self-rising) flour

1 Prepare a steamer or half fill a pan with water and bring it to the boil. Grease a 900ml/1½ pint/3¾ cup heatproof bowl and add half the walnuts.

2 Heat 50g/2oz/4 tbsp of the butter with 50g/2oz/4 tbsp of the sugar, the cream and 15ml/1 tbsp of the lemon juice in a small pan, stirring until smooth. Pour half the sauce into the greased bowl, then swirl to coat it a little way up the sides. Reserve the remaining sauce.

3 Beat the remaining butter and sugar until light and fluffy, then gradually beat in the eggs. Fold in the flour and the remaining nuts and lemon juice and spoon into the bowl.

4 Cover the bowl with baking parchment with a pleat folded in the centre, then tie securely with string. Steam the pudding for about 1¼ hours, topping up the boiling water as required, until it is set in the centre.

5 Just before serving, gently warm the remaining sauce. To serve, run a knife around the edge of the pudding to loosen it, then turn out on to a warm plate and pour over the sauce.

Cook's Tip
Putting a pleat in the paper cover allows room for the pudding to rise. Secure tightly to prevent water or steam entering.

Rice Pudding Energy 421Kcal/1786kJ; Protein 7.3g; Carbohydrate 95g, of which sugars 77g; Fat 3.4g, of which saturates 1g; Cholesterol 55mg; Calcium 195mg; Fibre 0.4g; Sodium 94mg.
Sticky Toffee Energy 571Kcal/2378kJ; Protein 7.3g; Carbohydrate 46g, of which sugars 31.6g; Fat 41.1g, of which saturates 18g; Cholesterol 131mg; Calcium 124mg; Fibre 1.3g; Sodium 275mg.

Tropical Fruit with Maple Butter

This dish turns exotic fruit
into comfort food.

Serves 4
1 large mango
1 large papaya
1 small pineapple
2 bananas
115g/4oz/½ cup unsalted
   (sweet) butter
60ml/4 tbsp pure maple syrup
ground cinnamon, for sprinkling

1 Peel the mango and cut the flesh into large pieces. Halve the papaya and scoop out the seeds. Cut into thick slices, then peel. Peel and core the pineapple and slice into thin wedges. Peel the bananas, then halve them lengthways.

2 Cut the butter into small dice and place in a blender or food processor with the maple syrup, then process until creamy.

3 Place the mango, papaya, pineapple and banana on a grill (broiler) rack and brush with the maple syrup butter. Cook under a medium heat for about 10 minutes, until just tender, turning the fruit occasionally and brushing it with the butter.

4 Arrange the fruit on a serving platter and dot with the remaining butter. Sprinkle over a little cinnamon and serve hot.

Variation/Tropical Fruits in Cinnamon Syrup
Sprinkle a third of 450g/1lb/2¼ cups caster (superfine) sugar over the base of a large pan. Add 1 cinnamon stick and half of the following: about 675g/1½lb papayas, peeled, seeded and cut into thin pieces; about 675g/1½lb mangoes, peeled, stoned (pitted) and cut lengthways into thin pieces; about 225g/8oz star fruit, thinly sliced. Sprinkle half the remaining sugar over the fruit pieces. Add the remaining fruit, sprinkled with the remaining sugar. Cover and cook over a medium-low heat for 35–45 minutes, until the sugar melts. Shake the pan occasionally, but do not stir (the fruit will collapse). Simmer, uncovered, for 10 minutes, until the fruit is becoming translucent. Remove from the heat and cool. Transfer to a bowl and chill, covered, overnight. Serve with yogurt or crème fraîche.

Blueberry Pancakes

These are rather like the
thick American breakfast
pancakes – though they can,
of course, be eaten at any
time of the day.

Makes 6–8
115g/4oz/1 cup self-raising
   (self-rising) flour
pinch of salt
45–60ml/3–4 tbsp caster
   (superfine) sugar
2 eggs
120ml/4fl oz/½ cup milk
15–30ml/1–2 tbsp oil
115g/4oz/1 cup fresh or frozen
   blueberries, plus extra
   to decorate
maple syrup, to serve
lemon wedges, to decorate

1 Sift the flour into a bowl with the salt and sugar. Beat together the eggs thoroughly. Make a well in the middle of the flour and stir in the eggs.

2 Gradually blend in a little of the milk to make a smooth batter. Then whisk in the rest of the milk and whisk for 1–2 minutes. Allow to rest for 20–30 minutes.

3 Heat a few drops of oil in a pancake pan or heavy frying pan until just hazy. Pour about 30ml/2 tbsp of the batter and swirl the batter around until it makes an even shape.

4 Cook for 2–3 minutes and when almost set on top, sprinkle over 15–30ml/1–2 tbsp blueberries. As soon as the base is loose and golden brown, turn the pancake over.

5 Cook on the second side for only about 1 minute, until golden and crisp. Slide the pancake on to a plate and serve drizzled with maple syrup. Continue with the rest of the batter. Serve decorated with lemon wedges and a few extra blueberries.

Cook's Tip
Instead of blueberries you could use blackberries or raspberries. If you use canned fruit, make sure it is very well drained.

Tropical Fruit Energy 470Kcal/1974kJ; Protein 2.7g; Carbohydrate 64g, of which sugars 62.7g; Fat 24.4g, of which saturates 15.1g; Cholesterol 61mg; Calcium 90mg; Fibre 7.7g; Sodium 229mg.
Blueberry Pancakes Energy 111Kcal/468kJ; Protein 3.5g; Carbohydrate 18.2g, of which sugars 7.5g; Fat 3.2g, of which saturates 0.8g; Cholesterol 48mg; Calcium 84mg; Fibre 0.9g; Sodium 76mg.

Apple Soufflé Omelette

Apples sautéed until they are slightly caramelized make a delicious autumn filling for these light-as-air sweet pancakes. Great for an impromptu supper.

Serves 2

4 eggs, separated
30ml/2 tbsp single (light) cream
15ml/1 tbsp caster (superfine) sugar

15g/½oz/1 tbsp butter
icing (confectioners') sugar, for dredging

For the filling

1 eating apple, peeled, cored and sliced
25g/1oz/2 tbsp butter
30ml/2 tbsp soft light brown sugar
45ml/3 tbsp single (light) cream

1 Make the filling. Sauté the apple slices in the butter and sugar until just tender. Stir in the cream and keep warm while making the omelette.

2 Place the egg yolks in a bowl with the cream and sugar and beat well. Whisk the egg whites until they form stiff peaks, then fold into the yolk mixture.

3 Melt the butter in a large heavy frying pan, pour in the soufflé mixture and spread evenly. Cook for 1 minute until golden underneath, then cover the pan handle with foil and place under a hot grill (broiler) to brown the top.

4 Slide the omelette on to a plate, add the apple mixture, then fold over. Sift the icing sugar over thickly, then mark in a criss-cross pattern with a hot metal skewer. Serve immediately.

Cook's Tips
• *When cooking the top, remove the omelette as soon as it is browned. Do not overcook at this stage otherwise the light texture of the omelette will be damaged.*
• *Try replacing the apples with fresh raspberries or strawberries when they are in season.*

Rhubarb-Strawberry Crisp

Strawberries, cinnamon and ground almonds make this a luxurious and delicious version of rhubarb crumble that's sure to go down well with all the family.

Serves 4

225g/8oz strawberries, hulled
450g/1lb rhubarb, diced
90g/3½oz/½ cup granulated sugar
15ml/1 tbsp cornflour (cornstarch)

85ml/3fl oz/⅓ cup fresh orange juice
115g/4oz/1 cup plain (all-purpose) flour
90g/3½oz/1 cup rolled oats
115g/4oz/½ cup light muscovado (brown) sugar
2.5ml/½ tsp ground cinnamon
50g/2oz/½ cup ground almonds
150g/5oz/10 tbsp cold butter
1 egg, lightly beaten
single (light) cream or natural (plain) yogurt, to serve

1 If the strawberries are large, cut them in half. Combine the strawberries, rhubarb and granulated sugar in a 2.4 litre/4 pint/10 cup baking dish. Preheat the oven to 180°C/350°F/Gas 4.

2 In a small bowl, blend the cornflour with the orange juice. Pour this mixture over the fruit and stir gently to coat. Set the baking dish aside while making the crumble topping.

3 In a bowl, toss together the flour, oats, muscovado sugar, cinnamon and ground almonds. With a pastry blender or two knives, cut in the butter until the mixture resembles coarse breadcrumbs. Stir in the beaten egg.

4 Spoon the oat mixture evenly over the fruit and press down gently. Cook in the oven for 50–60 minutes, until the top is golden brown. Serve warm with single cream or yogurt.

Cook's Tip
Rolled oats and ground almonds not only add interesting texture to the topping, but also turn this dish into a healthier version of traditional crumble.

Apple Omelette Energy 469Kcal/1952kJ; Protein 14.1g; Carbohydrate 27.5g, of which sugars 27.5g; Fat 34.8g, of which saturates 18.1g; Cholesterol 444mg; Calcium 107mg; Fibre 0.6g; Sodium 274mg.
Rh.-Strawb. Crisp Energy 808Kcal/3390kJ; Protein 11.8g; Carbohydrate 103g, of which sugars 60.9g; Fat 41.7g, of which saturates 20.5g; Cholesterol 128mg; Calcium 240mg; Fibre 5.6g; Sodium 269mg.

Blueberry Frangipane Flan

A lemon pastry case is filled with a sweet almond filling, dotted with blueberries.

Serves 6
30ml/2 tbsp ground coffee
45ml/3 tbsp milk
50g/2oz/¼ cup unsalted
  (sweet) butter
50g/2oz/¼ cup caster
  (superfine) sugar
1 egg
115g/4oz/1 cup ground almonds
15ml/1 tbsp plain

(all-purpose) flour, sifted
225g/8oz/2 cups blueberries
30ml/2 tbsp jam
15ml/1 tbsp brandy

For the pastry
175g/6oz/1½ cups plain
  (all-purpose) flour
115g/4oz/½ cup unsalted (sweet)
  butter or margarine
25g/1oz/2 tbsp caster
  (superfine) sugar
finely grated rind of ½ lemon
15ml/1 tbsp chilled water

1 Preheat the oven to 190°C/375°F/Gas 5. To make the pastry, sift the flour into a bowl and rub in the butter. Stir in the sugar and lemon rind, then add the water and mix to a firm dough. Wrap in clear film (plastic wrap) and chill for 20 minutes.

2 Roll out the pastry on a lightly floured work surface and use to line a 23cm/9in loose-based flan tin (tart pan). Line the pastry with baking parchment and baking beans and bake for 10 minutes. Remove the paper and beans and bake for a further 10 minutes. Remove from the oven.

3 Meanwhile, make the filling. Put the ground coffee in a bowl. Bring the milk almost to the boil, then pour over the coffee and leave to infuse for 4 minutes. Cream the butter and sugar until pale. Beat in the egg, then add the almonds and flour. Finely strain in the coffee-flavoured milk and fold in.

4 Spread the coffee mixture into the pastry case. Scatter the blueberries over and push down slightly into the mixture. Bake for 30 minutes, until firm, covering with foil after 20 minutes.

5 Heat the jam and brandy in a small pan until melted. Brush over the flan and remove from the tin.

Mango & Amaretti Strudel

Fresh mango and crushed amaretti wrapped in wafer-thin filo pastry make a special treat. The dessert looks impressive, but takes very little time to make.

Serves 4
1 large mango
grated rind of 1 lemon
2 amaretti
25g/1oz/2 tbsp demerara
  (raw) sugar

60ml/4 tbsp wholemeal
  (whole-wheat) breadcrumbs
2 sheets of filo pastry, each
  measuring 48 x 28cm/
  19 x 11in
25g/1oz/2 tbsp butter or
  20g/¾oz/4 tsp soft margarine,
  melted
15ml/1 tbsp chopped almonds
icing (confectioners') sugar,
  for dusting

1 Preheat the oven to 190°C/375°F/Gas 5. Lightly grease a baking sheet. Cut the flesh from the mango and chop into small cubes. Place in a bowl and sprinkle with the grated lemon rind.

2 Crush the amaretti and mix them with the sugar and breadcrumbs in a bowl.

3 Lay one sheet of filo pastry on a flat surface and brush with a quarter of the melted butter or margarine. Top with the second sheet, brush with one-third of the remaining fat, then fold both sheets over, if necessary, to make a rectangle measuring 28 x 24cm/11 x 9½in. Brush with half the remaining fat.

4 Sprinkle the filo with the amaretti mixture, leaving a border on each long side. Arrange the mango over the top.

5 Carefully roll up the filo from one long side, Swiss-roll (jelly-roll) fashion, to enclose the amaretti mixture. Lift the strudel on to the baking sheet, seam side down. Brush with the remaining melted fat and sprinkle with the chopped almonds.

6 Bake the strudel for 20–25 minutes until light golden brown, then transfer to a board. Dust with the icing sugar, slice diagonally and serve.

Flan Energy 523Kcal/2180kJ; Protein 8.9g; Carbohydrate 44.9g, of which sugars 20.2g; Fat 34.8g, of which saturates 15.6g; Cholesterol 91mg; Calcium 132mg; Fibre 3.6g; Sodium 188mg.
Strudel Energy 222Kcal/937kJ; Protein 4.2g; Carbohydrate 35.4g, of which sugars 13.4g; Fat 8.1g, of which saturates 3.6g; Cholesterol 13mg; Calcium 58mg; Fibre 2g; Sodium 162mg.

Peach Leaf Pie

Juicy, lightly spiced peach slices are covered with a crust made entirely from individual pastry leaves to make this spectacular pie.

Serves 8
1.2kg/2½lb ripe peaches
juice of 1 lemon
115g/4oz/½ cup granulated
  sugar
45ml/3 tbsp cornflour
  (cornstarch)
1.5ml/¼ tsp grated nutmeg
2.5ml/½ tsp ground cinnamon
25g/1oz/2 tbsp butter, diced
1 egg, beaten with 15ml/1 tbsp
  water, to glaze

For the pastry
225g/8oz/2 cups plain
  (all-purpose) flour
4ml/¾ tsp salt
115g/4oz/½ cup cold butter,
  diced
40g/1½oz/3 tbsp white vegetable
  fat, diced
75–90ml/5–6 tbsp chilled water

1 Make the pastry. Sift the flour and salt into a large mixing bowl. Add the butter and vegetable fat, and rub in with your fingertips or cut in with a pastry blender until the mixture resembles coarse breadcrumbs.

2 Sprinkle over the dry ingredients just enough of the water to bind the mixture and use a fork to bring it together to form a soft dough. Gather the dough into two balls, one slightly larger than the other. Wrap separately in clear film (plastic wrap) and chill for 30 minutes.

3 Meanwhile, put a baking sheet in the oven and preheat to 220°C/425°F/Gas 7.

4 Drop a few peaches at a time into a large pan of boiling water, leave for 20 seconds, then transfer to a bowl of cold water. When the peaches are cool, peel off the skins. Slice the peaches and mix with the lemon juice, sugar, cornflour and spices in a bowl. Set aside.

5 On a lightly floured surface, roll out the larger piece of pastry to a thickness of 3mm/⅛in. Use to line a 23cm/9in pie plate. Chill until required.

6 Roll out the second piece of pastry and cut out leaf shapes about 7.5cm/3in long. Cut out enough to completely cover the top of the dish. Mark veins with a knife.

7 Brush the base of the pastry case with egg glaze. Add the peach mixture, piling it into a dome in the centre. Dot the surface with the diced butter.

8 To assemble the pie top, start from the outside edge. Make a ring of leaves around the edge, attaching each leaf to the pastry base with a dab of egg glaze. Place a second ring of leaves above, staggering the positions. Continue with rows of leaves until the pie is covered. Brush with egg glaze.

9 Bake the pie on the hot baking sheet for about 10 minutes. Lower the oven temperature to 180°C/350°F/Gas 4 and continue to bake for 35–40 minutes more, or until golden. Serve hot with cream, if you wish.

Chocolate, Date & Almond Filo Coil

Experience the allure of the Middle East with this delectable dessert. Crisp filo pastry conceals a chocolate and rose water filling studded with dates and almonds.

Serves 6
275g/10oz filo pastry, thawed
  if frozen
50g/2oz/¼ cup butter, melted
icing (confectioners') sugar, cocoa
  powder (unsweetened) and
  ground cinnamon, for dusting

For the filling
75g/3oz/6 tbsp butter
115g/4oz dark (bittersweet)
  chocolate, broken up into pieces
115g/4oz/1⅓ cup ground
  almonds
115g/4oz/⅔ cup chopped dates
75g/3oz/⅔ cup icing
  (confectioners') sugar
10ml/2 tsp rose water
2.5ml/½ tsp ground cinnamon

1 Preheat the oven to 180°C/350°F/Gas 4. Grease a 22cm/8½in round cake tin (pan). To make the filling, melt the butter with the chocolate in a heatproof bowl set over a pan of barely simmering water, then remove from the heat and stir in the remaining ingredients to make a thick paste. Leave to cool.

2 Lay one sheet of filo on a clean, flat surface. Brush with melted butter, then lay a second sheet on top and brush with more butter.

3 Roll a handful of the chocolate and almond mixture into a long sausage shape and place along one long edge of the layered filo. Roll up the pastry tightly around the filling to make a roll.

4 Fit the filo roll in the cake tin, in such a way that it sits snugly against the outer edge. Make more filo rolls in the same way, adding them to the tin from the outside towards the centre, until the coil fills the tin.

5 Brush the coil with the remaining melted butter. Bake for 30–35 minutes until the pastry is golden brown and crisp. Transfer the coil to a serving plate. Serve warm, dusted with icing sugar, cocoa and cinnamon.

Peach Leaf Pie Energy 390Kcal/1638kJ; Protein 4.4g; Carbohydrate 53.8g, of which sugars 27.2g; Fat 19g, of which saturates 10.7g; Cholesterol 52mg; Calcium 62mg; Fibre 3.2g; Sodium 152mg.
Filo Coil Energy 543Kcal/2267kJ; Protein 8.2g; Carbohydrate 55.4g, of which sugars 32.4g; Fat 33.6g, of which saturates 15g; Cholesterol 46mg; Calcium 108mg; Fibre 3.2g; Sodium 133mg.

Bitter Chocolate Mousse

A classic and ever-popular dessert, little chocolate mousses make a stylish and memorable finish to any dinner party.

Serves 8
225g/8oz plain (semisweet) chocolate, chopped into small pieces
60ml/4 tbsp water
30ml/2 tbsp orange-flavoured liqueur or brandy
25g/1oz/2 tbsp unsalted (sweet) butter, cut into small pieces
4 eggs, separated
90ml/6 tbsp whipping cream
1.5ml/¼ tsp cream of tartar
45ml/3 tbsp caster (superfine) sugar
crème fraîche and chocolate curls, to decorate

1 Melt the chocolate with the water in a heatproof bowl set over a pan of barely simmering water, stirring until completely smooth. Remove from the heat and whisk in the liqueur or brandy and butter.

2 With a hand-held electric mixer, beat the egg yolks for 2–3 minutes until thick and creamy, then slowly beat into the melted chocolate until well blended. Set aside.

3 Whip the cream until soft peaks form and stir a spoonful into the chocolate mixture to lighten it. Fold in the remaining cream.

4 In a grease-free bowl, beat the egg whites slowly until frothy. Add the cream of tartar, increase the speed and continue beating until they form soft peaks. Gradually sprinkle over the sugar and continue beating until the whites are stiff and glossy.

5 Using a rubber spatula or large metal spoon, stir a quarter of the egg whites into the chocolate mixture, then gently fold in the remaining whites, cutting down to the bottom, along the sides and up to the top in a semicircular motion until they are just combined. Gently spoon into eight individual dishes. Chill for at least 2 hours or until set.

6 Spoon a little crème fraîche over each mousse and decorate with the chocolate curls.

Strawberry Cream Shortbreads

Simple to assemble, these pretty strawberry desserts are always popular. Serve them as soon as they are ready because the shortbread biscuits (cookies) will lose their lovely crisp texture if left to stand.

Serves 3
150g/5oz/generous 1 cup strawberries
450ml/¾ pint/scant 2 cups double (heavy) cream
6 round shortbread biscuits
fresh mint sprigs, to decorate (optional)

1 Reserve three strawberries for decoration. Hull the remaining strawberries and cut them in half.

2 Put the halved strawberries in a bowl and gently crush using the back of a fork. (Only crush the berries lightly; they should not be reduced to a purée.)

3 Put the cream in a large, clean bowl and whip to form soft peaks. Add the crushed strawberries and gently fold in to combine – do not overmix.

4 Halve the reserved strawberries, then spoon the strawberry and cream mixture on top of the shortbread biscuits. Decorate each one with half a strawberry and a mint sprig, if you like. Serve immediately.

Cook's Tip
Use whole strawberries for the decoration and give them a pretty frosted effect by painting with whisked egg white, then dipping in caster (superfine) sugar. Leave to dry before serving.

Variation
You can use any other berry you like for this dessert – try raspberries or blueberries. Two ripe, peeled peaches will also give great results.

Bitter Choc. Mousse Energy 276Kcal/1152kJ; Protein 4.8g; Carbohydrate 24.1g, of which sugars 23.9g; Fat 17.6g, of which saturates 9.9g; Cholesterol 115mg; Calcium 34mg; Fibre 0.7g; Sodium 61mg.
Shortbreads Energy 890Kcal/3673kJ; Protein 4.4g; Carbohydrate 22g, of which sugars 9.6g; Fat 87.8g, of which saturates 54.8g; Cholesterol 225mg; Calcium 105mg; Fibre 1g; Sodium 106mg.

White Chocolate Mousse with Dark Sauce

In this delicious dessert, creamy, white chocolate mousse is set off by a dark rum and chocolate sauce.

Serves 6–8

200g/7oz white chocolate, broken into squares
2 eggs, separated
60ml/4 tbsp caster (superfine) sugar
300ml/½ pint/1¼ cups double (heavy) cream
15ml/1 tbsp/1 sachet powdered gelatine
150ml/¼ pint/⅔ cup Greek (US strained plain) yogurt
10ml/2 tsp vanilla extract

For the sauce

50g/2oz plain (semisweet) chocolate, broken into squares
30ml/2 tbsp dark rum
60ml/4 tbsp single (light) cream

1 Line a 1 litre/1¾ pint/4 cup loaf tin (pan) with baking parchment or clear film (plastic wrap). Melt the chocolate in a heatproof bowl over hot water, then remove from the heat.

2 Whisk the egg yolks and sugar in a bowl until pale and thick, then beat in the melted chocolate.

3 Heat the cream in a small pan until almost boiling, then remove from the heat. Sprinkle the powdered gelatine over, stirring gently until it is completely dissolved. Then pour on to the chocolate mixture, whisking vigorously to mix until smooth.

4 Whisk the yogurt and vanilla extract into the mixture. In a clean, grease-free bowl, whisk the egg whites until stiff, then fold them into the mixture. Turn into the prepared loaf tin, level the surface and chill until set.

5 Make the sauce. Melt the chocolate with the rum and cream in a heatproof bowl over barely simmering water. Cool.

6 Remove the mousse from the tin with the aid of the lining. Serve sliced with the chocolate sauce poured around.

Rich Chocolate Mousse with Glazed Kumquats

Perfumed kumquats, glazed in orange liqueur, turn this mousse into a special treat.

Serves 6

225g/8oz plain (semisweet) chocolate, broken into squares
4 eggs, separated
30ml/2 tbsp orange-flavoured liqueur
90ml/6 tbsp double (heavy) cream

For the glazed kumquats

275g/10oz/2¾ cups kumquats
115g/4oz/generous ½ cup granulated sugar
150ml/¼ pint/⅔ cup water
15ml/1 tbsp orange-flavoured liqueur

1 To make the glazed kumquats, halve the fruit lengthways and place cut side up in a shallow serving dish.

2 Place the sugar in a small pan with the water. Heat gently, stirring constantly, until the sugar has dissolved, then bring to the boil and boil rapidly, without stirring, until a golden-brown caramel forms.

3 Remove the pan from the heat and very carefully stir in 60ml/4 tbsp boiling water. Stir in the orange-flavoured liqueur, then pour the caramel sauce over the kumquat slices and leave to cool. Once completely cold, cover and chill.

4 Line a shallow 20cm/8in round cake tin (pan) with clear film (plastic wrap). Melt the chocolate in a bowl over a pan of barely simmering water, then remove the bowl from the heat.

5 Beat the egg yolks and liqueur into the chocolate, then gently fold in the cream. In a separate mixing bowl, whisk the egg whites until stiff, then gently fold them into the chocolate mixture. Pour the mixture into the prepared tin and level the surface. Chill for several hours until set.

6 Turn the mousse out on to a plate and cut into slices. Serve with the glazed kumquats alongside.

White Choc. Mousse Energy 433Kcal/1796kJ; Protein 6g; Carbohydrate 25g, of which sugars 24.9g; Fat 34.4g, of which saturates 20.5g; Cholesterol 103mg; Calcium 133mg; Fibre 0.2g; Sodium 69mg.
Rich Choc. Mousse Energy 431Kcal/1805kJ; Protein 6.9g; Carbohydrate 49.8g, of which sugars 49.5g; Fat 22.3g, of which saturates 12.4g; Cholesterol 150mg; Calcium 71mg; Fibre 1.7g; Sodium 56mg.

Mocha Velvet Cream Pots

These dainty pots of chocolate heaven are a great way to round off a meal.

Serves 8
15ml/1 tbsp instant coffee
  powder
475ml/16fl oz/2 cups milk
75g/3oz/6 tbsp caster
  (superfine) sugar

225g/8oz plain (semisweet)
  chocolate, chopped into
  small pieces
10ml/2 tsp vanilla extract
30ml/2 tbsp coffee-flavoured
  liqueur (optional)
7 egg yolks
whipped cream and crystallized
  mimosa balls, to decorate

1 Preheat the oven to 160°C/325°F/Gas 3. Place eight 120ml/4fl oz/½ cup custard cups or ramekins in a roasting pan. Set the pan aside.

2 Put the instant coffee in a pan. Stir in the milk, then add the sugar and place the pan over medium heat. Bring to the boil, stirring constantly, until both the coffee and the sugar have dissolved completely.

3 Remove the pan from the heat and add the chocolate. Stir until it has melted and the sauce is smooth. Stir in the vanilla extract and coffee liqueur, if using.

4 In a bowl, whisk the egg yolks to blend them lightly. Slowly whisk in the chocolate mixture until well mixed, then strain the mixture into a large jug (pitcher) and divide equally among the cups or ramekins. Pour enough boiling water into the roasting pan to come halfway up the sides of the cups or ramekins. Carefully place the roasting pan in the oven.

5 Bake for 30–35 minutes, until the custard is just set and a knife inserted into the custard comes out clean. Remove the cups or ramekins from the roasting pan and allow to cool. Place on a baking sheet, cover and chill completely.

6 Decorate the pots with whipped cream and crystallized mimosa balls, if you wish.

Chocolate & Chestnut Pots

The chestnut purée adds substance and texture to these mousses. Crisp, delicate biscuits (cookies), such as langues-de-chat, provide a good foil to the richness.

Serves 6
250g/9oz plain (semisweet)
  chocolate
60ml/4 tbsp Madeira
25g/1oz/2 tbsp butter, diced
2 eggs, separated
225g/8oz/scant 1 cup
  unsweetened chestnut purée
crème fraîche or whipped double
  (heavy) cream, to decorate

1 Make a few chocolate curls for decoration by rubbing a grater along the length of the bar of chocolate. Break the rest of the chocolate into squares and melt it in a pan with the Madeira over a gentle heat. Remove from the heat and add the butter, a few pieces at a time, stirring until melted and smooth.

2 Beat the egg yolks quickly into the mixture, then beat in the chestnut purée, mixing until smooth.

3 Whisk the egg whites in a clean, grease-free bowl until stiff. Stir about 15ml/1 tbsp of the whites into the chestnut mixture to lighten it, then fold in the rest smoothly and evenly.

4 Spoon the mixture into six small ramekin dishes and chill until set.

5 Remove the pots from the refrigerator about 30 minutes before serving to allow the flavours to "ripen". Serve the pots topped with a generous spoonful of crème fraîche or whipped cream and decorated with chocolate curls.

> **Cook's Tips**
> • If Madeira is not available, use brandy or rum instead.
> • These chocolate pots can be frozen successfully for up to 2 months, making them ideal for a prepare-ahead dessert.

Mocha Velvet Energy 261Kcal/1095kJ; Protein 6g; Carbohydrate 30.5g, of which sugars 30.2g; Fat 13.7g, of which saturates 6.7g; Cholesterol 182mg; Calcium 106mg; Fibre 0.7g; Sodium 36mg.
Choc. & Chestnut Energy 348Kcal/1455kJ; Protein 5g; Carbohydrate 41.4g, of which sugars 29.9g; Fat 18g, of which saturates 9.9g; Cholesterol 75mg; Calcium 42mg; Fibre 2.6g; Sodium 56mg.

Coffee, Vanilla & Chocolate Stripe

This looks really special layered in wine glasses and decorated with cream.

Serves 6

285g/10½oz/1½ cups caster (superfine) sugar
90ml/6 tbsp cornflour (cornstarch)
900ml/1½ pints/3¾ cups milk
3 egg yolks
75g/3oz/6 tbsp unsalted (sweet) butter, at room temperature
20ml/generous 1 tbsp instant coffee powder
10ml/2 tsp vanilla extract
30ml/2 tbsp cocoa powder (unsweetened)

1 To make the coffee layer, place 90g/3½oz/½ cup of the sugar and 30ml/2 tbsp of the cornflour in a heavy pan. Gradually add one-third of the milk, whisking until well blended. Over a medium heat, whisk in one of the egg yolks and bring to the boil, whisking. Boil for 1 minute.

2 Remove the pan from the heat. Stir in 25g/1oz/2 tbsp of the butter and the instant coffee. Set aside the pan to cool slightly.

3 Divide the coffee mixture among six wine glasses. Smooth the tops before the mixture sets. Wipe any dribbles on the insides and outsides of the glasses with damp kitchen paper.

4 To make the vanilla layer, place half of the remaining sugar and cornflour in a heavy pan. Whisk in half the milk. Over a medium heat, whisk in another egg yolk and bring to the boil, whisking. Boil for 1 minute.

5 Remove the pan from the heat and stir in 25g/1oz/2 tbsp of the butter and the vanilla. Leave to cool slightly, then spoon into the glasses on top of the coffee layer. Smooth the tops.

6 To make the chocolate layer, place the remaining sugar and cornflour in a heavy pan. Gradually whisk in the remaining milk until blended. Over a medium heat, whisk in the last egg yolk and bring to the boil, whisking. Boil for 1 minute. Remove from the heat, stir in the remaining butter and the cocoa. Leave to cool slightly, then spoon on top of the vanilla layer. Chill to set.

Steamed Custard in Nectarines

Steaming nectarines or peaches brings out their natural colour and sweetness, so this is a good way of making the most of underripe or less flavourful fruit.

Serves 4–6

6 nectarines
1 large (US extra large) egg
45ml/3 tbsp palm sugar or light muscovado (brown) sugar
30ml/2 tbsp coconut milk

1 Cut the nectarines in half. Using a teaspoon, scoop out the stones (pits) and a little of the surrounding flesh.

2 Lightly beat the egg, then add the sugar and the coconut milk. Beat until the sugar has dissolved.

3 Transfer the nectarines to a steamer and carefully fill the cavities three-quarters full with the custard mixture. Steam over a pan of simmering water for 5–10 minutes. Remove from the heat and leave to cool completely before transferring to plates and serving.

Cook's Tip
Palm sugar, also known as jaggery, is made from the sap of certain Asian palm trees, such as coconut and palmyrah. It is available from Asian food stores. If you buy it as a cake or large lump, grate it before use.

Variations
• *To add extra colour to this dessert, drizzle the cold fruit with a raspberry sauce. To make the sauce, simply purée fresh raspberries, then press through a sieve (strainer) to remove the seeds. Sweeten with icing (confectioners') sugar to taste.*
• *Serve the nectarines with chocolate hazelnut rounds – melt some plain (semisweet) chocolate and spread on to circles drawn on baking parchment. Sprinkle with flaked (sliced) hazelnuts and leave to set. Remove from the paper and serve alongside.*

Chocolate Stripe Energy 448Kcal/1891kJ; Protein 7.9g; Carbohydrate 71.1g, of which sugars 56.8g; Fat 16.8g, of which saturates 9.6g; Cholesterol 136mg; Calcium 228mg; Fibre 0.6g; Sodium 203mg.
Steamed Custard Energy 103Kcal/438kJ; Protein 3.2g; Carbohydrate 21.6g, of which sugars 21.6g; Fat 1.1g, of which saturates 0.3g; Cholesterol 32mg; Calcium 21mg; Fibre 1.8g; Sodium 19mg.

Chocolate Pavlova with Passion Fruit Cream

This meringue dish has a delicious chewy centre that is hard to resist.

Serves 6
4 egg whites
200g/7oz/1 cup caster (superfine) sugar
20ml/4 tsp cornflour (cornstarch)
45g/1¾oz/3 tbsp cocoa powder (unsweetened)
5ml/1 tsp vinegar
chocolate leaves, to decorate

For the filling
150g/5oz plain (semisweet) chocolate, chopped into small pieces
250ml/8fl oz/1 cup double (heavy) cream
150g/5oz/⅔ cup Greek (US strained plain) yogurt
2.5ml/½ tsp vanilla extract
4 passion fruit

1 Preheat oven to 140°C/275°F/Gas 1. Cut a piece of baking parchment to fit a baking sheet. Draw on a 23cm/9in circle.

2 Whisk the egg whites in a clean, grease-free bowl until stiff. Gradually whisk in the sugar and continue to whisk until the mixture is stiff again. Whisk in the cornflour, cocoa and vinegar.

3 Place the baking parchment upside down on the baking sheet. Spread the mixture over the circle; make a slight dip in the centre. Bake for 1½–2 hours.

4 Make the filling. Melt the chocolate in a heatproof bowl over barely simmering water, then remove from the heat and cool slightly. In a separate bowl, whip the cream with the yogurt and vanilla extract until thick. Fold 60ml/4 tbsp into the chocolate, then set both mixtures aside.

5 Halve all the passion fruit and scoop out the pulp. Stir half into the plain cream mixture. Carefully transfer the meringue shell to a serving plate. Fill with the passion fruit cream, then spoon over the chocolate mixture and the remaining passion fruit pulp. Decorate with chocolate leaves. Serve immediately.

Meringue Squiggles

These delightful meringue shapes are easy to make, taste delicious and look fantastic. They're popular with children and adults alike and are great as a teatime treat or as a simple dessert with ice cream.

Makes 14–16
2 egg whites
90g/3½oz/scant ½ cup caster (superfine) sugar
multi-coloured sugar sprinkles, to decorate

1 Preheat the oven to 150°C/300°F/Gas 2. Line a large baking sheet with baking parchment.

2 Put the egg whites in a large bowl, reserving about 15ml/1 tbsp for decoration, and whisk until they form firm peaks. Add a spoonful of caster sugar and whisk briefly to combine. Add another spoonful and whisk again. Continue in this way until all the sugar has been incorporated.

3 Spoon the meringue mixture into a large piping (pastry) bag fitted with a large plain nozzle. Pipe wavy lines of meringue, about 13cm/5in long, on to the baking sheet and bake for about 1 hour, or until dry and crisp.

4 Carefully peel the meringues off the paper and transfer to a wire rack to cool.

5 Using a fine pastry brush, brush the tops of the meringues with the reserved egg white, then scatter over the multi-coloured sugar sprinkles to decorate.

> **Cook's Tip**
> If you prefer not to use raw egg white to decorate the meringue squiggles, use a sugar paste instead. Put 45g/1¾oz/3 tbsp icing (confectioners') sugar in a small bowl and add a few drops of water. Stir well to make a paste, then brush on to the meringues.

Pavlova Energy 541Kcal/2260kJ; Protein 7.3g; Carbohydrate 56.4g, of which sugars 52.3g; Fat 33.6g, of which saturates 20.4g; Cholesterol 59mg; Calcium 96mg; Fibre 1.9g; Sodium 146mg.
Meringue Squiggles Energy 24Kcal/101kJ; Protein 0.4g; Carbohydrate 5.9g, of which sugars 5.9g; Fat 0g, of which saturates 0g; Cholesterol 0mg; Calcium 3mg; Fibre 0g; Sodium 8mg.

Coffee Crêpes with Peaches & Cream

Summery peaches and brandy cream make a tasty filling for light crêpes.

Serves 6

75g/3oz/²⁄₃ cup plain
   (all-purpose) flour
25g/1oz/¹⁄₄ cup buckwheat flour
1 egg, beaten
200ml/7fl oz/scant 1 cup milk
15g/¹⁄₂oz/1 tbsp butter, melted
100ml/3¹⁄₂fl oz/scant ¹⁄₂ cup
   brewed coffee, cooled
sunflower oil, for frying

For the filling

6 ripe peaches
300ml/¹⁄₂ pint/1¹⁄₄ cups double
   (heavy) cream
15ml/1 tbsp brandy
225g/8oz/1 cup crème fraîche
65g/2¹⁄₂oz/5 tbsp unrefined
   caster (superfine) sugar
30ml/2 tbsp sifted icing
   (confectioners') sugar, for
   dusting (optional)

1 Sift the flours into a mixing bowl. Make a well in the middle and add the beaten egg, half the milk and the melted butter. Gradually mix in the flour, beating until the mixture is smooth, then beat in the remaining milk and the coffee.

2 Heat a drizzle of sunflower oil in a 15–20cm/6–8in crêpe pan. Pour in just enough batter to cover the base of the pan thinly, swirling the pan to spread the mixture evenly. Cook for 2–3 minutes until the underneath is golden brown, then flip the crêpe over using a metal spatula and cook the other side.

3 Slide the crêpe on to a plate. Continue making crêpes in this way, stacking and interleaving them with baking parchment.

4 To make the filling, halve the peaches and carefully remove the stones (pits). Cut the peaches into thick slices. Whip the cream and brandy together until soft peaks form. Beat the crème fraîche with the sugar until smooth. Beat 30ml/2 tbsp of the cream into the crème fraîche, then fold in the remainder.

5 Place the crêpes on plates. Spoon a little of the brandy cream on to one half of each crêpe and top with peach slices. Fold the crêpe over and dust with a little icing sugar, if you wish.

Devilish Chocolate Roulade

Indulge yourself with this wickedly rich roulade.

chocolate-dipped strawberries, to
   decorate

Serves 6–8

175g/6oz plain (semisweet)
   chocolate, chopped into
   small pieces
4 eggs, separated
115g/4oz/generous ¹⁄₂ cup caster
   (superfine) sugar
cocoa powder (unsweetened),
   for dusting

For the filling

225g/8oz plain (semisweet)
   chocolate, chopped into
   small pieces
45ml/3 tbsp brandy
2 eggs, separated
250g/9oz/generous 1 cup
   mascarpone

1 Preheat oven to 180°C/350°F/Gas 4. Grease a 33 × 23cm/ 13 × 9in Swiss roll tin (jelly roll pan) and line with baking parchment. Melt the chocolate in a bowl over a pan of hot water.

2 Whisk the egg yolks and sugar in a bowl until pale and thick, then stir in the melted chocolate. Place the egg whites in a clean, grease-free bowl. Whisk them to soft peaks, then fold lightly and evenly into the egg and chocolate mixture.

3 Scrape into the tin and spread to the corners. Bake for 15–20 minutes, until well risen and firm to the touch. Dust a sheet of baking parchment with cocoa. Turn the sponge out on to the paper, cover with a clean dish towel and cool.

4 Make the filling. Melt the chocolate with the brandy in a heatproof bowl over a pan of simmering water. Remove from the heat. Beat the egg yolks together, then beat into the chocolate mixture. In a separate bowl, whisk the whites to soft peaks, then fold them lightly and evenly into the filling.

5 Uncover the roulade, remove the lining paper and spread with the mascarpone. Spread the chocolate mixture over the top, then roll up carefully from a long side to enclose the filling. Transfer to a serving plate with the join underneath, top with fresh chocolate-dipped strawberries and chill before serving.

Crêpes Energy 578Kcal/2403kJ; Protein 6.5g; Carbohydrate 36.3g, of which sugars 23.1g; Fat 45.7g, of which saturates 28.8g; Cholesterol 150mg; Calcium 123mg; Fibre 2.1g; Sodium 63mg.
Roulade Energy 486Kcal/2022kJ; Protein 10.2g; Carbohydrate 32.8g, of which sugars 32.4g; Fat 34.5g, of which saturates 19.9g; Cholesterol 189mg; Calcium 41mg; Fibre 1.3g; Sodium 143mg.

An Ice Bowl for a Sorbet

Nothing sets off a freshly scooped sorbet quite so effectively as an ice bowl inlaid with fresh flowers and leaves. Ice bowls are easy to make, inexpensive and stunning enough to grace any special celebration, from lunch party to country wedding.

Serves 8–10

ice cubes
cold water
selection of fresh edible flowers
*   and leaves*
18–20 scoops of sorbet, to serve

1 Place some ice cubes in the base of a 3.5 litre/6 pint/15 cup clear plastic or glass freezerproof bowl. Tuck some flowers and leaves around the ice. Position a smaller bowl so that it rests on the ice cubes, leaving an even space between the two bowls.

2 Pour cold water into the space between the bowls until the water level starts to come up the sides. Freeze for 2–3 hours until frozen.

3 Tuck more flowers and leaves between the two bowls, mixing the flowers and leaves so that they look attractive through the sides of the larger bowl.

4 Place some kitchen weights or food cans in the central bowl to stop it from rising, then fill the space between the bowls to the rim with more water. Freeze overnight until firm.

5 Release the inner bowl by pouring boiling water into it almost to the top. Quickly tip out the water and lift away the inner bowl. Repeat the process if the bowl won't come free instantly.

6 To remove the outer bowl, dip it quickly in a large bowl of very hot water until the ice bowl loosens. Return the ice bowl to the freezer.

7 Shortly before serving, scoop the sorbet into the bowl. Return to the freezer until ready to serve.

Lavender & Honey Ice Cream

Lavender and honey make a memorable partnership in this old-fashioned and elegant ice cream. Serve scooped into glasses or set in little moulds and top with lightly whipped cream. Pretty lavender flowers add the finishing touch.

Serves 6–8

90ml/6 tbsp clear honey
4 egg yolks
10ml/2 tsp cornflour (cornstarch)
8 lavender sprigs, plus extra
*   to decorate*
450ml/¾ pint/scant 2 cups milk
450ml/¾ pint/scant 2 cups
*   whipping cream*
thin biscuits (cookies), to serve

1 Put the honey, egg yolks, and cornflour in a bowl. Separate the lavender flowers from the stalks and add them with a little milk. Whisk lightly. Bring the remaining milk to the boil in a heavy pan. Add to the egg yolk mixture, stirring well.

2 Return the mixture to the pan and cook very gently, stirring until the mixture thickens. Pour the custard into a bowl, cover the surface closely with a circle of waxed paper and leave to cool, then chill until very cold.

3 Whip the cream and fold into the custard. Pour into a freezer container and freeze for 3–4 hours, beating twice as it thickens. Return to the freezer until ready to serve.

4 Alternatively, use an ice cream maker. Stir the cream into the custard, then churn the mixture until it holds its shape. Transfer to a freezer container and freeze until ready to serve.

5 Transfer the ice cream to the refrigerator 30 minutes before serving, so that it softens slightly. Scoop into small dishes, decorate with lavender flowers and serve with biscuits.

> **Cook's Tip**
> *To make lavender sugar for flavouring desserts, leave some lavender in caster (superfine) sugar, then sieve before using.*

Sorbet Energy 73Kcal/308kJ; Protein 0.2g; Carbohydrate 18.6g, of which sugars 17.5g; Fat 0.2g, of which saturates 0g; Cholesterol 0mg; Calcium 6mg; Fibre 0g; Sodium 8mg.
Ice Cream Energy 308Kcal/1275kJ; Protein 4.5g; Carbohydrate 13.9g, of which sugars 12.8g; Fat 26.4g, of which saturates 15.6g; Cholesterol 163mg; Calcium 113mg; Fibre 0g; Sodium 45mg.

Spicy Pumpkin & Orange Bombe

In this fabulous bombe dessert, a mouthwatering pumpkin ice cream is encased in delicious sponge and served with an orange and whole-spice syrup.

Serves 8

115g/4oz/½ cup unsalted (sweet) butter or margarine, softened
115g/4oz/generous ½ cup caster (superfine) sugar
115g/4oz/1 cup self-raising (self-rising) flour
2.5ml/½ tsp baking powder
2 eggs

For the ice cream

450g/1lb fresh pumpkin, seeded and cubed
1 orange
300g/11oz/scant 1½ cups granulated sugar
300ml/½ pint /1¼ cups water
2 cinnamon sticks, halved
10ml/2 tsp whole cloves
30ml/2 tbsp orange flower water
300ml/½ pint/1¼ cups extra-thick double (heavy) cream
2 pieces preserved stem ginger, grated
icing (confectioners') sugar, for dusting

1 Preheat the oven to 180°C/350°F/Gas 4. Grease and base-line a 450g/1lb loaf tin (pan).

2 Make the sponge. Beat the butter or margarine, caster sugar, flour, baking powder and eggs in a bowl until creamy. Spoon the mixture into the prepared tin, then level the surface and bake for 30–35 minutes until firm in the centre. Leave in the tin for a few minutes then turn out and cool.

3 Make the ice cream. Steam the cubes of pumpkin for about 15 minutes, or until tender. Drain and blend in a food processor to form a smooth purée. Leave to cool.

4 Pare thin strips of rind from the orange, then cut into very fine shreds. Squeeze the orange and set the juice aside. Heat the sugar and water in a small, heavy pan until the sugar dissolves. Boil rapidly without stirring for 3 minutes.

5 Stir in the orange shreds and juice, cinnamon and cloves and heat gently for 5 minutes. Strain the syrup, reserving the orange shreds and spices. Measure 300ml/½ pint/1¼ cups of the syrup and reserve. Return the spices to the remaining syrup and stir in the orange flower water. Pour into a jug (pitcher) and cool.

6 Beat the pumpkin purée with 175ml/6fl oz/¾ cup of the measured strained syrup until evenly combined. Stir in the cream and ginger. Cut the cake into 1cm/½in slices. Dampen a 1.5 litre/2½ pint/6¼ cup deep bowl and line it with clear film (plastic wrap). Pour the remaining strained syrup into a shallow dish.

7 Dip the cake slices briefly in the syrup and use to line the prepared bowl, placing the coated sides against the bowl.

8 Pour the pumpkin mixture into a shallow container and freeze until firm. Scrape the ice cream into the sponge-lined bowl, level the surface and freeze until firm, preferably overnight.

9 To serve, invert the bombe on to a plate. Lift off the bowl and clear film. Dust with the icing sugar and serve with the spiced syrup spooned over.

Classic Dark Chocolate Ice Cream

Rich, dark and wonderfully luxurious, this ice cream can be served solo or drizzled with warm chocolate sauce. If you are making it in advance, don't forget to soften the ice cream before serving so that the full flavour of the chocolate comes through.

Serves 4–6

4 egg yolks
75g/3oz/6 tbsp caster (superfine) sugar
5ml/1 tsp cornflour (cornstarch)
300ml/½ pint/1¼ cups semi-skimmed (low-fat) milk
200g/7oz dark (bittersweet) chocolate
300ml/½ pint/1¼ cups whipping cream
shaved chocolate, to decorate

1 Whisk the egg yolks, sugar and cornflour in a bowl until thick and foamy. Pour the milk into a pan, bring just to the boil, then gradually whisk it into the yolk mixture.

2 Return the mixture to the pan and cook over a gentle heat, stirring constantly until the custard thickens and is smooth. Remove the pan from the heat.

3 Break the chocolate into small pieces and stir into the hot custard until it has melted. Leave to cool, then chill.

4 Whip the cream until it has thickened but still falls from a spoon. Fold into the custard, then pour into a freezer container. Freeze for 6 hours or until firm enough to scoop, beating once or twice with a fork or in a food processor as it thickens.

5 Alternatively, use an ice cream maker. Mix the chocolate custard with the whipped cream. Churn until firm enough to scoop. Serve in scoops, decorated with chocolate shavings.

Cook's Tip

For the best flavour use a good-quality chocolate with at least 75 per cent cocoa solids, such as fine Belgian chocolate.

Pumpkin Bombe Energy 571Kcal/2387kJ; Protein 4.2g; Carbohydrate 67g, of which sugars 56.1g; Fat 33.6g, of which saturates 20.5g; Cholesterol 130mg; Calcium 122mg; Fibre 1g; Sodium 168mg.
Choc. Ice Cream Energy 349Kcal/1461kJ; Protein 4.8g; Carbohydrate 36.8g, of which sugars 35.8g; Fat 21.4g, of which saturates 11.9g; Cholesterol 162mg; Calcium 78mg; Fibre 0.7g; Sodium 29mg.

White Chocolate Castles

These impressive and romantic-looking chocolate cases serve a wide variety of uses. They can be frozen with iced mousses or other desserts set in them, or, as in this recipe, filled with scoops of ice cream and succulent fresh blueberries.

Serves 6
225g/8oz white chocolate, broken into pieces
250ml/8fl oz/1 cup white chocolate ice cream
250ml/8fl oz/1 cup dark (bittersweet) chocolate ice cream
115g/4oz/1 cup blueberries
cocoa powder (unsweetened), for dusting

1 Put the white chocolate in a heatproof bowl, set it over a pan of gently simmering water and leave until melted. Line a baking sheet with baking parchment. Cut out six 30 x 13cm/12 x 5in strips of baking parchment, then fold each in half lengthways.

2 Stand a 7.5cm/3in pastry cutter on the baking sheet. Roll one strip of paper into a circle and fit inside the cutter with the folded edge on the base paper. Stick the edges together with tape.

3 Remove the cutter and make more paper collars in the same way, leaving the pastry cutter in place around the final collar.

4 Spoon a little of the melted chocolate into the base of the collar supported by the cutter. Using a teaspoon, spread the chocolate over the base and up the sides of the collar, making the top edge uneven. Carefully lift away the cutter.

5 Make five more chocolate cases in the same way, using the cutter for extra support each time. Leave the cases in a cool place or in the refrigerator to set.

6 Carefully peel away the paper from the sides of the chocolate cases then lift the cases off the base. Transfer to serving plates.

7 Using a teaspoon, scoop the ice creams into the cases and decorate with the fruit. Dust with cocoa powder and serve.

Strawberry Semi-Freddo

Serve this quick strawberry and ricotta dessert semi-frozen to enjoy the flavour at its best. The contrasting texture of crisp dessert biscuits (cookies) makes the perfect accompaniment.

Serves 4–6
250g/9oz/generous 2 cups strawberries
115g/4oz/scant ½ cup strawberry jam
250g/9oz/generous 1 cup ricotta cheese
200g/7oz/scant 1 cup Greek (US strained plain) yogurt
5ml/1 tsp natural vanilla extract
40g/1½oz/3 tbsp caster (superfine) sugar
extra strawberries and mint or lemon balm, to decorate

1 Put the strawberries in a bowl and mash them with a fork until broken into small pieces but not completely puréed. Stir in the strawberry jam. Drain off any whey from the ricotta.

2 Transfer the ricotta to a large bowl and stir in the Greek yogurt, vanilla extract and sugar. Using a dessertspoon, gently fold the mashed strawberries into the ricotta mixture to create a rippled effect.

3 Spoon into individual freezerproof dishes and freeze for at least 2 hours until almost solid. Alternatively, freeze until completely solid, then transfer the ice cream to the refrigerator for about 45 minutes to soften before serving.

4 Serve in small bowls with extra strawberries and decorated with mint or lemon balm.

> **Cook's Tip**
> Don't mash the strawberries too much or they'll become too liquid. Freeze in a large freezer container if you don't have suitable small dishes. Transfer to the refrigerator to thaw slightly, then scoop into glasses.

Choc. Castles Energy 351Kcal/1463kJ; Protein 6g; Carbohydrate 34.3g, of which sugars 34.2g; Fat 22g, of which saturates 13.1g; Cholesterol 0mg; Calcium 182mg; Fibre 1.2g; Sodium 84mg.
Semi-Freddo Energy 181Kcal/764kJ; Protein 5.8g; Carbohydrate 29.6g, of which sugars 29.6g; Fat 5.3g, of which saturates 3.2g; Cholesterol 15mg; Calcium 91mg; Fibre 0.9g; Sodium 43mg.

Nectarine & Hazelnut Meringues

If it's indulgence you're seeking, look no further. Sweet nectarines and cream syllabub paired with crisp hazelnut meringues make a superb dessert that is quite irresistible.

Serves 5
3 egg whites
150g/5oz/¾ cup caster (superfine) sugar
50g/2oz/½ cup chopped hazelnuts, toasted
300ml/½ pint/1¼ cups double (heavy) cream
60ml/4 tbsp sweet dessert wine
2 nectarines, stoned (pitted) and sliced
fresh mint sprigs, to decorate

1 Preheat the oven to 140°C/275°F/Gas 1. Line two large baking sheets with baking parchment.

2 Whisk or beat the egg whites in a grease-free bowl until they form stiff peaks when the whisk or beaters are lifted. Gradually whisk in the caster sugar, a spoonful at a time, until the mixture forms a stiff, glossy meringue.

3 Fold in two-thirds of the chopped toasted hazelnuts, then spoon five large ovals on to each lined baking sheet. Sprinkle the remaining hazelnuts over five of the meringue ovals. Flatten the tops of the remaining five ovals.

4 Bake the meringues for 1–1¼ hours until crisp and dry, then carefully lift them off the baking parchment and leave them to cool completely on a wire rack.

5 Whip the cream with the dessert wine until the mixture forms soft peaks. Spoon some of the cream syllabub on to each of the plain meringues. Arrange a few nectarine slices on top of each syllabub-topped meringue.

6 Place each meringue on a dessert plate and add a hazelnut-topped meringue to each plate. Decorate the portions with mint sprigs and serve immediately.

Chocolate Meringues with Mixed Fruit Compote

A glamorous dinner party dessert that is hard to beat.

blackcurrants, redcurrants, raspberries and blackberries

Serves 6
105ml/7 tbsp unsweetened red grape juice
105ml/7 tbsp unsweetened apple juice
30ml/2 tbsp clear honey
450g/1lb/4 cups mixed fresh summer berries, such as

For the meringues
3 egg whites
150g/5oz/¾ cup caster (superfine) sugar
75g/3oz good-quality plain (semisweet) chocolate, finely grated
175g/6oz/¾ cup crème fraîche

1 Preheat the oven to 110°C/225°F/Gas ¼. Grease and line two large baking sheets with baking parchment, cutting the paper to fit.

2 Make the meringues. Whisk the egg whites in a large mixing bowl until stiff. Gradually whisk in half the sugar, then fold in the remaining sugar, using a metal spoon. Gently fold in the grated plain chocolate. Carefully spoon the meringue mixture into a large piping (pastry) bag fitted with a large star nozzle. Pipe small round whirls of the mixture on to the prepared baking sheets.

3 Bake the meringues for 2½–3 hours until they are firm and crisp. Remove from the oven. Carefully peel the meringues off the paper, then transfer them to a wire rack to cool.

4 Meanwhile, make the compote. Heat the fruit juices and honey in a pan until the mixture is almost boiling. Place the mixed berries in a large bowl and pour over the hot fruit juice and honey mixture. Stir gently to mix, then set aside and leave to cool. Once cool, cover the bowl with clear film (plastic wrap) and chill until required.

5 To serve, sandwich the cold meringues together with crème fraîche. Spoon the mixed fruit compote on to individual plates, top with the meringues and serve immediately.

Nect. & Hazel. Energy 540Kcal/2250kJ; Protein 5.1g; Carbohydrate 43.8g, of which sugars 43.6g; Fat 38.6g, of which saturates 20.5g; Cholesterol 82mg; Calcium 68mg; Fibre 1.3g; Sodium 54mg.
Choc. Meringues Energy 343Kcal/1442kJ; Protein 4g; Carbohydrate 50.2g, of which sugars 50g; Fat 15.4g, of which saturates 10.1g; Cholesterol 34mg; Calcium 61mg; Fibre 2.2g; Sodium 44mg.

Iced Christmas Torte

This makes an exciting alternative to traditional Christmas pudding – but don't feel that you have to limit it to the festive season.

Serves 8–10

75g/3oz/³⁄₄ cup dried cranberries
75g/3oz/scant ¹⁄₂ cup pitted prunes
50g/2oz/¹⁄₃ cup sultanas (golden raisins)
175ml/6fl oz/³⁄₄ cup port
2 pieces preserved stem ginger, finely chopped
25g/1oz/2 tbsp unsalted (sweet) butter
45ml/3 tbsp light muscovado (brown) sugar
90g/3¹⁄₂oz/scant 2 cups fresh white breadcrumbs
600ml/1 pint/2¹⁄₂ cups double (heavy) cream
30ml/2 tbsp icing (confectioners') sugar
5ml/1 tsp ground allspice
75g/3oz/³⁄₄ cup brazil nuts, finely chopped
sugared bay leaves and fresh cherries, to decorate

1 Put the cranberries, prunes and sultanas in a food processor and process briefly. Transfer them to a bowl and add the port and ginger. Leave to absorb the port for 2 hours.

2 Melt the butter in a frying pan. Add the sugar and heat gently until the sugar has dissolved. Add the breadcrumbs, stir lightly, then fry over a low heat for about 5 minutes, until lightly coloured and turning crisp. Leave to cool.

3 Turn the breadcrumbs into a food processor or blender and process to finer crumbs. Sprinkle a third into an 18cm/7in loose-based springform tin (pan) and freeze.

4 Whip the cream with the icing sugar and spice until the mixture is thick but not yet standing in peaks. Fold in the brazil nuts with the dried fruit mixture and any port remaining.

5 Spread a third of the mixture over the breadcrumb base in the tin, taking care not to dislodge the crumbs. Sprinkle with another layer of the breadcrumbs. Repeat the layering, finishing with a layer of the cream mixture. Freeze the torte overnight. Serve decorated with sugared bay leaves and fresh cherries.

Chocolate & Brandied Fig Torte

A seriously rich torte for chocolate lovers. If you dislike figs, use dried prunes, dates or apricots instead.

Serves 8

250g/9oz/1¹⁄₂ cups dried figs
60ml/4 tbsp brandy
200g/7oz gingersnap biscuits (cookies)
175g/6oz/³⁄₄ cup unsalted (sweet) butter, softened
150ml/¹⁄₄ pint/²⁄₃ cup milk
250g/9oz plain (semisweet) chocolate, broken into pieces
45ml/3 tbsp caster (superfine) sugar
cocoa powder (unsweetened), for dusting
whipped cream, to serve

1 Chop the figs and put them into a bowl, pour over the brandy and leave for 2–3 hours until most of the brandy has been absorbed. Break the biscuits into large chunks, put them in a strong plastic bag and crush them with a rolling pin.

2 Melt half the butter and stir in the crumbs until combined. Pack on to the bottom and up the sides of a 20cm/8in loose-based flan tin (tart pan) that is about 3cm/1¹⁄₄in deep. Leave in the refrigerator to chill.

3 Pour the milk into a pan, add the chocolate pieces and heat gently until the chocolate has melted and the mixture is smooth, stirring frequently. Pour the chocolate mixture into a bowl and leave to cool.

4 In a separate bowl, beat the remaining butter with the caster sugar until the mixture is pale and creamy.

5 Add the chocolate mixture, whisking until it is well mixed. Fold in the figs, and any remaining brandy, and spoon the mixture into the chilled flan case. Level the surface, cover and freeze overnight.

6 Transfer the frozen torte to the refrigerator about 30 minutes before serving so that the filling softens slightly. Lightly dust the surface with cocoa powder and serve in slices, with dollops of lightly whipped cream.

Christmas Torte Energy 504Kcal/2098kJ; Protein 6.3g; Carbohydrate 38.4g, of which sugars 21g; Fat 36.4g, of which saturates 17.8g; Cholesterol 61mg; Calcium 92mg; Fibre 2.3g; Sodium 209mg.
Choc. & Fig Torte Energy 539Kcal/2257kJ; Protein 5g; Carbohydrate 63.9g, of which sugars 54.2g; Fat 29.7g, of which saturates 17.7g; Cholesterol 50mg; Calcium 172mg; Fibre 4.1g; Sodium 241mg.

Rhubarb & Ginger Wine Torte

The classic combination of rhubarb and ginger is used in this luxury frozen torte to make a dessert with a refreshingly tart flavour.

Serves 8
500g/1¼lb rhubarb, trimmed
115g/4oz/generous ½ cup caster (superfine) sugar
30ml/2 tbsp water
200g/7oz/scant 1 cup cream cheese
150ml/¼ pint/⅔ cups double (heavy) cream
40g/1½oz/¼ cup preserved stem ginger, finely chopped
a few drops of pink food colouring (optional)
250ml/8fl oz/1 cup ginger wine
175g/6oz sponge fingers
fresh mint or lemon balm sprigs, dusted with icing sugar, to decorate

1 Chop the rhubarb roughly and put it in a pan with the sugar and water. Cover and cook very gently for 5–8 minutes until the rhubarb is just tender. Process in a food processor or blender until smooth, then leave to cool.

2 Beat the cheese in a bowl until softened. Stir in the cream, rhubarb purée and ginger, then food colouring, if you like. Line a 900g/2lb/6–8 cup loaf tin (pan) with clear film (plastic wrap).

3 Pour the mixture into a shallow freezer container and freeze until firm. Alternatively, churn in an ice cream maker.

4 Pour the ginger wine into a shallow dish. Spoon a thin layer of ice cream over the bottom of the tin. Working quickly, dip the sponge fingers in the ginger wine, then lay them lengthways over the ice cream in a single layer, trimming to fit.

5 Spread another layer of ice cream over the top. Repeat the process, adding two to three more layers and finishing with ice cream. Cover and freeze overnight.

6 Transfer to the refrigerator 30 minutes before serving, to soften the torte slightly. To serve, briefly dip in very hot water then invert on to a flat dish. Peel off the lining and decorate.

Frozen Grand Marnier Soufflés

These sophisticated little desserts make a wonderful end to a meal.

Serves 8
200g/7oz/1 cup caster (superfine) sugar
6 large (US extra large) eggs, separated
250ml/8fl oz/1 cup milk
15g/½oz powdered gelatine, soaked in 45ml/3 tbsp cold water
45ml/3 tbsp water
450ml/¾ pint/scant 2 cups double (heavy) cream
60ml/4 tbsp Grand Marnier

1 Tie a double collar of waxed paper around eight ramekin dishes. Put 75g/3oz/6 tbsp of the sugar in a bowl with the egg yolks and whisk until pale.

2 Heat the milk until almost boiling and pour it on to the yolks, whisking all the time. Return the egg mixture to the pan and stir over a gentle heat until thick enough to coat the spoon.

3 Remove the pan from the heat and stir in the soaked gelatine. Pour into a bowl and leave to cool. Whisk occasionally, until it is on the point of setting.

4 Put the remaining sugar in a pan with the water and dissolve it over a low heat. Bring to the boil and boil rapidly until it reaches the soft ball stage or 119°C/238°F on a sugar thermometer. Remove from the heat.

5 In a clean bowl, whisk the egg whites until they are stiff. Pour the hot syrup on to the whites, whisking constantly. Set aside and leave to cool.

6 Whisk the cream until it holds soft peaks. Add the Grand Marnier to the cold custard and fold the custard into the cold meringue mixture, with the cream. Quickly pour into the prepared ramekin dishes. Freeze overnight.

7 Remove the paper collars. Leave the soufflés at room temperature for 30 minutes before serving.

Rhubarb & Ginger Energy 398Kcal/1658kJ; Protein 3.9g; Carbohydrate 29.4g, of which sugars 25.2g; Fat 26.8g, of which saturates 16.2g; Cholesterol 100mg; Calcium 132mg; Fibre 1.2g; Sodium 111mg.
Grand Marnier Energy 478Kcal/1991kJ; Protein 6.7g; Carbohydrate 33.7g, of which sugars 33.7g; Fat 34.9g, of which saturates 20.3g; Cholesterol 222mg; Calcium 99mg; Fibre 0g; Sodium 79mg.

Luxury Dark Chocolate Ravioli

Serve this special treat with cream and grated chocolate.

Serves 4
175g/6oz/1½ cups plain (all-purpose) flour
25g/1oz/¼ cup cocoa powder (unsweetened)
salt

30ml/2 tbsp icing (confectioners') sugar
2 large eggs, beaten
15ml/1 tbsp olive oil

For the filling
175g/6oz white chocolate, chopped
350g/12oz/1½ cups cream cheese
1 egg, plus 1 beaten egg to seal

1 Make the pasta. Sift the flour with the cocoa, salt and icing sugar on to a work surface. Make a well in the centre and pour in the eggs and oil. Mix together with your fingers. Knead until smooth. Cover and rest for at least 30 minutes.

2 For the filling, melt the white chocolate in a heatproof bowl placed over a pan of simmering water. Cool slightly. Beat the cream cheese in a bowl, then beat in the chocolate and egg. Spoon into a piping (pastry) bag fitted with a plain nozzle.

3 Cut the dough in half and wrap one portion in clear film (plastic wrap). Roll the pasta out thinly to a rectangle on a lightly floured surface, or use a pasta machine. Cover with a clean damp dish towel and repeat with the remaining pasta.

4 Pipe small mounds (about 5ml/1 tsp) of filling in rows, spacing them at 4cm/1½in intervals across one piece of the dough. Brush the dough between the mounds with beaten egg.

5 Using a rolling pin, lift the remaining sheet of pasta over the dough with the filling. Press down firmly between the pockets of filling, pushing out any trapped air. Cut the filled chocolate pasta into rounds with a ravioli cutter or sharp knife. Transfer to a floured dish towel. Leave for 1 hour to dry out.

6 Bring a frying pan of water to the boil and add the ravioli a few at a time, stirring to prevent sticking. Simmer gently for 3–5 minutes, remove with a perforated spoon and serve.

Chocolate Amaretto Marquise

This wickedly rich chocolate dessert is truly extravagant.

Serves 10–12
15ml/1 tbsp flavourless vegetable oil, such as groundnut (peanut) or sunflower
75g/3oz/7–8 amaretti, finely crushed
25g/1oz/¼ cup unblanched almonds, toasted and finely chopped
450g/1lb fine-quality plain or dark (bittersweet) chocolate, chopped into small pieces

75ml/5 tbsp Amaretto di Saronno liqueur
75ml/5 tbsp golden (light corn) syrup
475ml/16fl oz/2 cups double (heavy) cream
cocoa powder (unsweetened), for dusting

For the Amaretto cream
350ml/12fl oz/1½ cups whipping cream or double (heavy) cream
30–45ml/2–3 tbsp Amaretto di Saronno liqueur

1 Lightly oil a 23cm/9in heart-shaped or springform cake tin (pan). Line the bottom with baking parchment, then oil the paper. In a small bowl, combine the crushed amaretti and the chopped almonds. Sprinkle evenly on to the base of the tin.

2 Place the chocolate, Amaretto liqueur and golden syrup in a medium pan over a very low heat. Stir frequently until the chocolate has melted and the mixture is smooth. Remove from the heat and allow it to cool for about 6–8 minutes, until the mixture feels just warm to the touch.

3 Whip the cream until it just begins to hold its shape. Stir a large spoonful into the chocolate mixture, to lighten it, then quickly add the remaining cream and gently fold in. Pour into the prepared tin, on top of the amaretti mixture. Level the surface. Cover the tin with clear film (plastic wrap) and chill overnight.

4 To unmould, run a slightly warmed, thin-bladed sharp knife around the edge of the dessert, then unmould. Carefully peel off the paper, replacing any crust that sticks to it, and dust with cocoa. In a bowl, whip the cream and Amaretto liqueur to soft peaks. Serve separately.

Ravioli Energy 894Kcal/3722kJ; Protein 16.2g; Carbohydrate 68.1g, of which sugars 34g; Fat 63.9g, of which saturates 36.5g; Cholesterol 226mg; Calcium 299mg; Fibre 2.1g; Sodium 424mg.
Choc. Marquise Energy 589Kcal/2444kJ; Protein 3.9g; Carbohydrate 38.2g, of which sugars 35.1g; Fat 46.4g, of which saturates 27.5g; Cholesterol 87mg; Calcium 63mg; Fibre 1.2g; Sodium 57mg.

Chocolate Puffs

Cream-filled choux pastry puffs are an exquisite treat.

Serves 4–6
65g/2½oz/9 tbsp plain (all-
   purpose) flour
150ml/¼ pint/⅔ cup water
50g/2oz/¼ cup butter
2 eggs, beaten

For the filling and icing
150ml/¼ pint/⅔ cup double
   (heavy) cream
225g/8oz/1½ cups icing
   (confectioners') sugar
15ml/1 tbsp cocoa powder
   (unsweetened)
30–60ml/2–4 tbsp water

1 Preheat the oven to 220°C/425°F/Gas 7. Sift the flour into a bowl. Put the water in a pan over a medium heat, add the butter and heat gently until it melts. Increase the heat and bring to the boil, then remove from the heat. Add all the flour at once and beat quickly until the mixture sticks together and becomes thick and glossy, leaving the side of the pan clean. Leave the mixture to cool slightly.

2 Add the eggs, a little at a time, to the mixture and beat by hand with a wooden spoon or with an electric whisk, until the mixture (choux pastry) is thick and glossy and drops reluctantly from a spoon. (You may not need to use all of the egg.) Spoon the choux pastry into a piping (pastry) bag fitted with a 2cm/¾in nozzle. Dampen two baking sheets with cold water.

3 Pipe walnut-size spoonfuls of the choux pastry on to the dampened baking sheets. Leave some space for them to rise. Cook for 25–30 minutes, until they are golden brown and well risen. Use a palette knife to lift the puffs on to a wire rack, and make a small hole in each one with the handle of a wooden spoon to allow the steam to escape. Leave to cool.

4 Make the filling and icing. Whip the cream until thick. Put it into a piping bag fitted with a plain or star nozzle. Push the nozzle into the hole in each puff and squirt a little cream inside. Put the icing sugar and cocoa in a small bowl and stir together. Add enough water to make a thick glossy icing. Spread a little icing on each puff and serve when set.

Strawberry & Kirsch Choux Ring

This spectacular ring is made from individual balls of choux pastry.

Serves 4–6
350g/12oz/generous 2 cups small
   whole strawberries
75g/3oz/6 tbsp granulated sugar
150ml/¼ pint/⅔ cup double
   (heavy) cream
30ml/2 tbsp Kirsch

10ml/2 tsp icing (confectioners')
   sugar, sifted, plus extra for
   dusting
whipped cream, to serve

For the pastry
150ml/¼ pint/⅔ cup water
50g/2oz/¼ cup butter
65g/2½oz/9 tbsp plain
   (all-purpose) flour, sifted
2 eggs, beaten

1 Preheat the oven to 220°C/425°F/Gas 7. Reserve half the strawberries and slice the rest. Draw a 15cm/6in circle on a sheet of parchment. Turn it over and press on to a greased baking sheet.

2 Make the pastry. Heat the water and butter in a pan until the butter melts, bring to the boil, add the flour and remove from the heat. Beat with a wooden spoon until the mixture forms a ball, leaving the pan-sides clean. Gradually beat in the eggs to form a smooth paste. Spoon/pipe the pastry in balls, making a circle on the baking sheet, using the drawn circle. The balls should just touch each other. Bake for 15 minutes, then lower the heat to 190°C/375°F/Gas 5 and cook for 20–25 minutes. Make one or two slits in the pastry to let the hot air escape. Leave to cool.

3 Heat the granulated sugar until it dissolves, then increase the heat and cook the syrup until it turns a gold colour and a spoonful hardens when dropped into a bowl of cold water. Using a fork, half-dip and turn each whole strawberry in the syrup. Leave the strawberries to cool on baking parchment.

4 Make the filling. Whip the cream in a bowl until it just starts to thicken. Stir in the Kirsch and icing sugar and continue whisking until stiff. With a wooden spoon, fold in the sliced strawberries. Slice the choux ring in half horizontally, spoon in the strawberry cream and replace the top. Dust with a little icing sugar. Serve with whipped cream and the dipped strawberries.

Choc. Puffs Energy 403Kcal/1687kJ; Protein 4.2g; Carbohydrate 48.4g, of which sugars 39.8g; Fat 22.8g, of which saturates 13.6g; Cholesterol 115mg; Calcium 62mg; Fibre 0.6g; Sodium 106mg.
Choux Ring Energy 324Kcal/1346kJ; Protein 4.1g; Carbohydrate 25.5g, of which sugars 17.2g; Fat 22.3g, of which saturates 13.2g; Cholesterol 115mg; Calcium 54mg; Fibre 1g; Sodium 84mg.

Ice Cream Croissants with Chocolate Sauce

A deliciously easy-to-make croissant "sandwich" with a tempting filling of vanilla custard, ice cream and chocolate sauce melting inside the warmed bread.

Makes 4

75g/3oz plain (semisweet) chocolate, broken into pieces
15g/½oz/1 tbsp unsalted (sweet) butter
30ml/2 tbsp golden (light corn) syrup
4 croissants
90ml/6 tbsp good quality ready-made vanilla custard
4 large scoops of vanilla ice cream
icing (confectioners') sugar, for dusting

1 Preheat the oven to 180°C/350°F/Gas 4. Put the chocolate in a small, heavy pan. Add the butter and syrup and heat very gently until smooth, stirring the mixture frequently.

2 Split each of the croissants in half horizontally and place the base halves on a baking sheet. Spoon over the ready-made custard so that it covers the croissant bases, cover with the lids and bake in the oven for approximately 5 minutes or until warmed through.

3 Remove the lids and place a scoop of ice cream in each croissant. Spoon half the chocolate sauce over the ice cream and press the lids down gently. Put the croissants in the oven for 1 minute more.

4 Dust the filled croissants with icing sugar, spoon over the remaining chocolate sauce and serve immediately.

> **Variation**
> Add a dash of brandy to the chocolate sauce and use coffee-flavoured ice cream instead of vanilla.

Sicilian Brioche with Hot Fudge Sauce

For sheer indulgence, this dessert is unbeatable. Warm brioche filled with ice cream and topped with a glorious hot fudge sauce will make anyone's day.

Serves 2

2 individual brioches
2 large scoops of best vanilla or coffee ice cream

For the hot fudge sauce
50g/2oz best dark (bittersweet) chocolate with 70% cocoa solids
15g/½oz/1 tbsp butter
75ml/5 tbsp boiling water
30ml/2 tbsp golden (light corn) syrup
150g/5oz/¾ cup soft light brown sugar, sifted
5ml/1 tsp vanilla extract

1 Preheat the oven to 200°C/400°F/Gas 6. Meanwhile, make the hot fudge sauce. Break up the chocolate and place in a heatproof bowl set over a pan of barely simmering water. Leave, without stirring, for about 10 minutes until the chocolate has completely melted, then stir in the butter.

2 Add the boiling water to the melted chocolate and butter, stir well to blend, then stir in the syrup, sugar and vanilla extract. Pour and scrape the chocolate mixture into a pan and bring to the boil, then turn down the heat and allow to barely bubble for 5 minutes.

3 Meanwhile, put the brioches on a baking sheet and warm them in the oven for approximately 5 minutes – or until they are slightly crisp on the outside but are still soft, fluffy and warm on the inside.

4 Remove the pan of chocolate sauce from the heat. Immediately split the brioches open and gently pull out a little of the insides. Generously fill each brioche base with ice cream and gently press on the tops.

5 Put the filled brioches into individual bowls or on to plates and pour over the hot fudge sauce. Serve immediately.

Brioche Energy 913Kcal/3853kJ; Protein 13.8g; Carbohydrate 163.3g, of which sugars 121.5g; Fat 27.2g, of which saturates 15.4g; Cholesterol 18mg; Calcium 257mg; Fibre 3g; Sodium 674mg.
Croissants Energy 498Kcal/2086kJ; Protein 8.7g; Carbohydrate 59.4g, of which sugars 35g; Fat 29.5g, of which saturates 14.6g; Cholesterol 55mg; Calcium 134mg; Fibre 1.5g; Sodium 341mg.

Coffee Profiteroles

Irresistible coffee-flavoured choux puffs, with a liqueur-laced white chocolate sauce.

Serves 6
65g/2½oz/9 tbsp plain
  (all-purpose) flour
pinch of salt
50g/2oz/4 tbsp butter, diced
150ml/¼ pint/⅔ cup freshly
  brewed coffee
2 eggs, lightly beaten

250ml/8fl oz/1 cup double (heavy)
  cream, whipped

For the white chocolate sauce
50g/2oz/¼ cup granulated sugar
120ml/4fl oz/½ cup water
150g/5oz white chocolate, broken
  into pieces
25g/1oz/2 tbsp unsalted (sweet)
  butter
45ml/3 tbsp double (heavy) cream
30ml/2 tbsp coffee liqueur

1 Preheat the oven to 220°C/425°F/Gas 7. Sift the flour and salt on to a piece of baking parchment.

2 Place the butter in a pan with the coffee. Bring to a rolling boil, then remove from the heat and pour in the sifted flour in one go. Beat hard until the mixture leaves the side of the pan, forming a ball of thick paste. Leave to cool for 5 minutes.

3 Gradually add the eggs, beating well after each addition, until the mixture forms a stiff dropping consistency. Spoon into a piping (pastry) bag fitted with a 1cm/½in plain nozzle. Pipe 24 small buns on a dampened baking sheet, leaving plenty of room between them. Bake for 20 minutes, until risen.

4 Remove the buns from the oven and pierce the side of each one with a sharp knife to let out the steam.

5 Make the sauce. Put the sugar and water in a heavy pan, and heat gently until the sugar has completely dissolved. Bring to the boil and simmer for 3 minutes. Remove the pan from the heat, and add the white chocolate and butter, stirring constantly until smooth. Stir in the double cream and liqueur.

6 Spoon the whipped cream into a piping bag and fill the choux buns through the slits. Serve with the sauce poured over.

Iced Strawberry & Lemon Gâteau

Perfect for summer entertaining, this glorious iced gâteau is layered with favourite fruit flavours.

Serves 8
115g/4oz/½ cup unsalted (sweet)
  butter, softened
115g/4oz/generous ½ cup caster
  (superfine) sugar
2 eggs
115g/4oz/1 cup self-raising
  (self-rising) flour
2.5ml/½ tsp baking powder

To finish
500ml/17fl oz/2¼ cups
  strawberry ice cream
300ml/½ pint/1¼ cups double
  (heavy) cream
200g/7oz/scant 1 cup
  good-quality lemon curd
30ml/2 tbsp lemon juice
500g/1¼lb/5 cups strawberries,
  hulled
25g/1oz/2 tbsp caster (superfine)
  sugar
45ml/3 tbsp Cointreau or other
  orange-flavoured liqueur

1 Preheat the oven to 180°C/350°F/Gas 4. Grease and line a 23cm/9in round springform cake tin (pan). In a bowl, beat the butter with the sugar, eggs, flour and baking powder until creamy.

2 Spoon the mixture into the prepared tin and bake for about 20 minutes or until just firm. Leave to cool for 5 minutes, then turn the cake out on a wire rack. Cool completely.

3 Line the sides of the cleaned cake tin with a strip of baking parchment. Using a sharp knife, carefully slice off the top of the cake where it has formed a crust. Save this for another use.

4 Fit the cake in the tin, cut-side down. Freeze the cake for 10 minutes, then cover with the ice cream and freeze until firm.

5 Whip the cream in a bowl until it forms soft peaks, then fold in the lemon curd and lemon juice. Spoon the mixture over the strawberry ice cream. Cover and freeze overnight.

6 About 45 minutes before serving, cut half the strawberries into thin slices. Purée the rest of the strawberries with the sugar and liqueur to make the sauce. Arrange the sliced strawberries over the frozen gâteau. Serve with the sauce.

Profiteroles Energy 577Kcal/2393kJ; Protein 6g; Carbohydrate 34.3g, of which sugars 26g; Fat 46.4g, of which saturates 28.1g; Cholesterol 157mg; Calcium 123mg; Fibre 0.3g; Sodium 139mg.
Gâteau Energy 653Kcal/2725kJ; Protein 6.5g; Carbohydrate 66.8g, of which sugars 49.9g; Fat 40.2g, of which saturates 24.6g; Cholesterol 150mg; Calcium 164mg; Fibre 1.2g; Sodium 224mg.

Mini Praline Pavlovas

Melt-in-the-mouth meringue topped with rich, velvety chocolate and nutty praline.

Makes 14
2 large (US extra large) egg whites
large pinch of ground cinnamon
90g/3½oz/½ cup caster (superfine) sugar
50g/2oz/½ cup pecan nuts, finely chopped

For the filling
50g/2oz/¼ cup unsalted (sweet) butter, diced
100g/3½oz/scant 1 cup icing (confectioners') sugar, sifted
50g/2oz plain (semisweet) chocolate, broken into pieces

For the praline
50g/2oz/¼ cup caster (superfine) sugar
15g/½oz/1 tbsp finely chopped toasted almonds

1 Preheat the oven to 140°C/275°F/Gas 1. Line two baking sheets with baking parchment. Whisk the egg whites until stiff. Stir the cinnamon into the sugar. Add a spoonful of sugar to the egg whites and whisk well. Continue whisking in the sugar, a spoonful at a time, until thick and glossy. Stir in the pecan nuts.

2 Place 14 spoonfuls of meringue on the prepared baking sheets, well spaced. Using the back of a wet teaspoon, make a small hollow in the top of each meringue. Bake in the oven for 45–60 minutes until dry and just beginning to colour. Cool.

3 Make the filling. Beat together the butter and icing sugar until light and creamy. Place the chocolate in a heatproof bowl. Set over a pan of barely simmering water and stir occasionally until melted. Cool the chocolate slightly, then add to the butter mixture and stir well. Divide the filling among the meringues.

4 Make the praline. Put the sugar in a small non-stick frying pan. Heat gently until the sugar melts to form a clear liquid. When the mixture begins to turn brown, stir in the nuts. When the mixture is a golden brown, remove from the heat and pour immediately on to a lightly oiled or non-stick baking sheet. Leave to cool completely and then break into small pieces. Sprinkle over the meringues and serve.

Dark Chocolate & Hazelnut Tart

The crisp, hazelnut-flavoured pastry tastes wonderful combined with a luxurious chocolate filling.

Serves 10
300ml/½ pint/1¼ cups double (heavy) cream
150ml/¼ pint/⅔ cup creamy milk
150g/5oz dark (bittersweet) chocolate, chopped
4 eggs
50g/2oz/¼ cup caster (superfine) sugar
5ml/1 tsp vanilla extract
15ml/1 tbsp plain (all-purpose) flour

115g/4oz/1 cup toasted hazelnuts
10ml/2 tsp icing (confectioners') sugar, for dusting

For the pastry
150g/5oz/1¼ cups plain (all-purpose) flour
pinch of salt
40g/1½oz/3 tbsp caster (superfine) sugar
50g/2oz/½ cup ground hazelnuts, toasted
90g/3½oz/scant ½ cup butter, diced
1 egg, lightly beaten

1 Make the pastry. Sift the flour, salt and sugar into a mixing bowl, then mix in the toasted hazelnuts. Rub or cut in the butter until the mixture resembles fine breadcrumbs.

2 Make a well in the centre, add the beaten egg and mix to a firm dough. Knead the dough on a lightly floured surface for a few seconds until smooth. Wrap in clear film (plastic wrap) and chill for 30 minutes.

3 Roll out the pastry on a floured surface and use to line a 23cm/9in loose-based heart-shaped flan tin (tart pan). Trim the edges. Cover and chill for a further 30 minutes.

4 Re-roll the pastry trimmings into a long strip, about 30cm/12in long. Cut this into six strips, each 5mm/¼in wide, and make two plaits (braids) with three pastry strips in each. Curve into a heart shape and press gently to join together at both ends. Carefully place the heart on a baking sheet lined with baking parchment, and chill.

5 Put a baking sheet in the oven and preheat to 200°C/400°F/Gas 6. Prick the base of the pastry case (pie shell) with a fork. Line with foil and baking beans and bake blind on the sheet for 10 minutes. Remove the foil and beans and bake for a further 5 minutes. Bake the pastry plait on the shelf below for 10 minutes, or until lightly browned.

6 Meanwhile, pour the cream and milk into a pan and bring to the boil. Add the chocolate and stir until melted. Whisk the eggs, caster sugar, vanilla and flour together in a bowl. Pour the hot chocolate cream over the egg mixture, whisking all the time. Stir in the chopped hazelnuts.

7 Pour the chocolate and hazelnut mixture into the pastry case and bake in the oven for 25 minutes, or until just set. Allow the tart to cool, then remove from the tin and transfer to a serving plate. Place the pastry rope on top of the tart, then lightly dust the surface with icing sugar.

Praline Cakes Energy 148Kcal/621kJ; Protein 1.3g; Carbohydrate 21.2g, of which sugars 21.1g; Fat 7g, of which saturates 2.7g; Cholesterol 8mg; Calcium 16mg; Fibre 0.3g; Sodium 32mg.
Hazelnut Tart Energy 544Kcal/2261kJ; Protein 8.8g; Carbohydrate 35.6g, of which sugars 22.5g; Fat 41.8g, of which saturates 19.2g; Cholesterol 158mg; Calcium 105mg; Fibre 2g; Sodium 106mg.

Syrupy Brioche Slices with Vanilla Ice Cream

Keep a few individual brioche rolls in the freezer so that you can whip them out to make this fabulous five-minute pudding.

Serves 4
butter, for greasing
finely grated rind and juice of
  1 orange
50g/2oz/¼ cup caster
  (superfine) sugar
90ml/6 tbsp water
1.5ml/¼ tsp ground
  cinnamon
4 brioche rolls
15ml/1 tbsp icing (confectioners')
  sugar
400ml/14fl oz/1⅔ cups vanilla
  ice cream

1 Lightly grease a shallow flameproof dish and set aside. Put the orange rind and juice, sugar, water and cinnamon in a heavy pan. Heat gently, stirring, until the sugar has dissolved, then boil for 2 minutes without stirring.

2 Remove the syrup from the heat and pour it into a heatproof shallow dish. Preheat the grill (broiler).

3 Cut each brioche vertically into three thick slices. Dip one side of each brioche slice in the hot syrup and arrange in the greased flameproof dish, with the syrup-coated sides down. Reserve the remaining syrup. Grill (broil) the brioche until lightly toasted.

4 Turn over and dust with icing sugar. Grill for 2–3 minutes more until they begin to caramelize around the edges.

5 Transfer to individual plates and top with scoops of ice cream. Spoon over the remaining syrup and serve immediately.

Cook's Tip
For a slightly more tart taste, use grated lemon rind in the recipe instead of the orange rind.

Marbled Caramel Chocolate Slice

This classic recipe is made even more special here with a decorative marbled chocolate topping.

Makes about 24
250g/9oz/2¼ cups plain
  (all-purpose) flour
75g/3oz/6 tbsp caster (superfine)
  sugar
175g/6oz/¾ cup unsalted (sweet)
  butter, softened

For the filling
90g/3½oz/scant ½ cup unsalted
  (sweet) butter, diced
90g/3½oz/½ cup light
  muscovado (brown) sugar
two 397g/14oz cans evaporated
  (unsweetened condensed) milk

For the topping
90g/3½oz plain (semisweet)
  chocolate
90g/3½oz milk chocolate
50g/2oz white chocolate

1 Preheat the oven to 180°C/350°F/Gas 4. Line and lightly grease a 33 × 23cm/13 × 9in Swiss roll tin (jelly roll pan). Put the flour and sugar in a bowl and rub in the butter until the mixture resembles fine breadcrumbs, then form into a dough.

2 Press the dough over the base of the tin. Prick all over with a fork and bake for about 20 minutes, or until firm to the touch and very light brown. Set aside and leave in the tin to cool.

3 Make the filling. Put the butter, muscovado sugar and milk in a pan and heat gently, stirring, until the sugar has dissolved. Simmer the mixture very gently, stirring constantly, for about 5–10 minutes, or until it has thickened and has turned a caramel colour. Remove from the heat.

4 Pour the filling mixture over the pastry base, spread evenly, then leave until cold.

5 Make the topping. Melt each type of chocolate separately in a microwave or in a heatproof bowl set over hot water. Spoon lines of plain and milk chocolate over the set caramel filling.

6 Add small spoonfuls of white chocolate. Use a skewer to form a marbled effect on the topping.

Brioche Slices Energy 409Kcal/1725kJ; Protein 8.5g; Carbohydrate 68.4g, of which sugars 45.3g; Fat 12g, of which saturates 7.2g; Cholesterol 25mg; Calcium 175mg; Fibre 1.3g; Sodium 251mg.
Marbled Slice Energy 305Kcal/1279kJ; Protein 4.5g; Carbohydrate 39.8g, of which sugars 31.8g; Fat 15.3g, of which saturates 9.5g; Cholesterol 36mg; Calcium 125mg; Fibre 0.5g; Sodium 117mg.

Indian Kulfi Ice Cream

This famous Indian ice cream is traditionally made by slowly boiling milk until it has reduced to about one-third of the original quantity. Although you can save time by using condensed milk, nothing beats this delicious ice cream when made in the authentic manner.

Serves 4
1.5 litres/2½ pints/6¼ cups milk
3 cardamom pods
25g/1oz/2 tbsp caster (superfine) sugar
50g/2oz/½ cup pistachio nuts, skinned, plus a few to decorate
a few pink rose petals, to decorate

1 Pour the milk into a large, heavy pan. Bring to the boil, lower the heat and simmer gently for 1 hour, stirring occasionally.

2 Put the cardamom pods in a mortar and crush them with a pestle. Add the pods and the seeds to the milk and continue to simmer for 1–1½ hours or until the milk has reduced to about 475ml/16fl oz/2 cups.

3 Strain the flavoured milk into a jug (pitcher), stir in the sugar and leave to cool.

4 Grind half the pistachio nuts to a smooth powder in a blender, nut grinder or cleaned coffee grinder. Cut the remaining pistachios into thin slivers and reserve for decoration. Stir the ground nuts into the milk mixture.

5 Pour the milk and pistachio mixture into four kulfi moulds. (If you do not have suitable moulds, use plastic cups instead.) Freeze overnight until firm.

6 To unmould the kulfi, half fill a plastic container or bowl with very hot water, stand the moulds in the water and count to ten. Immediately lift out the moulds and invert them on to a baking sheet to turn out the ice creams.

7 Transfer the ices to a platter or individual plates. Scatter sliced pistachios and rose petals over the top and serve immediately.

Italian Coffee Granita

Very popular in Italy, a granita is a cross between a frozen drink and a flavoured ice. The consistency should be slushy, not solid. Granitas are simple to make at home with the help of a food processor.

Serves 4–5
475ml/16fl oz/2cups water
115g/4oz/½ cup granulated sugar
250ml/8fl oz/1 cup very strong espresso coffee, cooled
whipped cream, to garnish (optional)

1 Heat the water with the sugar over low heat until the sugar dissolves. Bring to the boil, then remove from the heat and allow to cool.

2 Combine the coffee with the sugar syrup. Place in a shallow freezer container and freeze until solid.

3 Plunge the bottom of the frozen container into very hot water for a few seconds. Turn the frozen mixture out and chop it into large chunks.

4 Place the mixture in a food processor fitted with a metal blade, and process until it forms small crystals. Spoon the granita into individual bowls or glasses and top with whipped cream, if you like.

Variation/Lemon Granita
Heat 475ml/16fl oz/2 cups water with 115g/4oz/½ cup granulated sugar over low heat until the sugar dissolves. Bring to the boil. Remove from the heat, and cool. Combine the juice and grated rind of 1 lemon (scrubbed before grating) with the sugar syrup. Place in a shallow container or freezer tray and freeze until solid. Plunge the bottom of the frozen container into very hot water for a few seconds. Turn the frozen mixture out, then chop it into chunks. Process the mixture in a metal-bladed food processor until it forms small crystals. Serve immediately, spooned into individual serving dishes.

Coffee Granita Energy 93Kcal/396kJ; Protein 0.6g; Carbohydrate 24.2g, of which sugars 24g; Fat 0g, of which saturates 0g; Cholesterol 0mg; Calcium 16mg; Fibre 0g; Sodium 4mg.
Kulfi Ice Cream Energy 347Kcal/1443kJ; Protein 14.7g; Carbohydrate 24.4g, of which sugars 24.1g; Fat 21.6g, of which saturates 10.4g; Cholesterol 53mg; Calcium 460mg; Fibre 0.8g; Sodium 228mg.

Iced Tiramisu

This favourite Italian combination is not usually served as a frozen dessert, but in fact it does make a marvellous ice cream.

Serves 4
150g/5oz/¾ cup caster (superfine) sugar
150ml/¼ pint/⅔ cup water
250g/9oz/generous 1 cup mascarpone
200g/7oz/scant 1 cup virtually fat-free fromage frais or cream cheese
5ml/1 tsp vanilla extract
10ml/2 tsp instant coffee, dissolved in 30ml/2 tbsp boiling water
30ml/2 tbsp coffee liqueur or brandy
75g/3oz sponge fingers
cocoa powder (unsweetened) and chocolate curls, to decorate

1 Put 115g/4oz/generous ½ cup of the sugar into a small pan. Add the water and bring to the boil, stirring until the sugar has dissolved. Leave the syrup to cool, then chill.

2 Put the mascarpone into a bowl. Beat with a spoon until it is soft, then stir in the fromage frais. Add the chilled sugar syrup, a little at a time, then stir in the vanilla extract.

3 Spoon the mixture into a freezer container and freeze for 4 hours, beating twice with a fork, electric whisk or in a food processor to break up the ice crystals. Alternatively, use an ice cream maker and churn the mascarpone mixture until it is thick but too soft to scoop.

4 Meanwhile, put the coffee in a bowl, sweeten with the remaining sugar, then add the liqueur. Stir well, then cool. Crumble the sponge fingers and toss in the coffee mixture.

5 Spoon a third of the ice cream into a 900ml/1½ pint/3¾ cup freezer container, spoon over half the crumbled sponge, then top with half the remaining ice cream. Sprinkle over the rest of the crumbled sponge, then cover with the remaining ice cream.

6 Freeze for 2–3 hours until firm enough to scoop. Serve dusted with cocoa powder and decorated with chocolate curls.

Dondurma Kaymalki

This sweet, pure white ice cream comes from the Middle East, where it is traditionally thickened with sahlab and flavoured with orange flower water and mastic, a resin used in chewing gum. As sahlab and mastic are both difficult to obtain in the West, cornflour and condensed milk have been used in this delicious version.

Serves 4–6
45ml/3 tbsp cornflour (cornstarch)
600ml/1 pint/2½ cups milk
213g/7½oz can sweetened condensed milk
15ml/1 tbsp clear honey
10ml/2 tsp orange flower water
a few sugared almonds, to serve

1 Put the cornflour in a pan and mix to a smooth paste with a little of the milk. Stir in the remaining milk and the condensed milk and bring the mixture to the boil, stirring until it has thickened and is smooth. Pour the mixture into a bowl.

2 Stir in the honey and orange flower water. Cover with a plate to prevent a skin forming, leave to cool, then chill.

3 Pour the mixture into a freezer container and freeze for 6–8 hours, beating twice with a fork, electric whisk or in a food processor to break up the ice crystals.

4 Alternatively, use an ice cream maker and churn the mixture until firm enough to scoop.

5 To serve, scoop the ice cream into dishes and serve with a few sugared almonds.

Cook's Tip
If you have made the ice cream by hand, transfer it to the refrigerator 30 minutes before you are ready to scoop. Rose water can be used instead of orange flower water.

Kaymalki Energy 218Kcal/917kJ; Protein 6.4g; Carbohydrate 33g, of which sugars 26.1g; Fat 7.5g, of which saturates 4.8g; Cholesterol 27mg; Calcium 222mg; Fibre 0g; Sodium 97mg.
Iced Tiramisu Energy 362Kcal/1526kJ; Protein 11.7g; Carbohydrate 54.5g, of which sugars 50.3g; Fat 10.5g, of which saturates 6.1g; Cholesterol 69mg; Calcium 78mg; Fibre 0.2g; Sodium 35mg.

Classic Italian Tiramisu

Tiramisu has become one of the principal desserts that people associate with Italy, its birthplace. The word "tiramisu" actually means "pick me up" in Italian and this rich coffee dessert is guaranteed to do just that. Tiramisu has many variations, with the only constant ingredient being the mascarpone, but this particular recipe is certainly a tasty version.

Serves 6–8

500g/1¼lb mascarpone
5 eggs, separated, at room
  temperature
90g/3½oz/½ cup caster
  (superfine) sugar
pinch of salt
savoyard or sponge fingers, for
  lining
120ml/4fl oz/½ cup strong
  espresso coffee
60ml/4 tbsp brandy or rum
  (optional)
cocoa powder (unsweetened),
  to sprinkle

1 Beat the mascarpone in a small bowl until soft. In a separate bowl, beat the egg yolks with the sugar (reserving 15ml/1 tbsp) until the mixture is pale yellow and fluffy. Gradually beat in the softened mascarpone.

2 Using an electric whisk or wire whisk, beat the egg whites with the salt until they form stiff peaks. Fold the egg whites into the mascarpone mixture.

3 Line one large or 6–8 individual serving dishes with a layer of sponge fingers.

4 Add the reserved sugar to the coffee, and stir in the brandy or rum, if using.

5 Sprinkle the coffee over the sponge lining: it should be moist but not saturated. Cover with half of the egg mixture. Add a layer of sponge fingers moistened with coffee, and cover with the remaining egg mixture.

6 Sprinkle with cocoa powder. Chill for at least 1 hour, preferably more, before serving.

Zabaglione

This airy Italian egg dish, fortified with sweet wine, is a traditional old Italian favourite. Said to have originated in the Venice region, it is usually eaten warm with biscuits (cookies) or fruit. If you serve it with fruit, then strawberries or raspberries are especially good choices.

Serves 3–4

3 egg yolks
40g/1½oz/3 tbsp caster
  (superfine) sugar
75ml/5 tbsp Marsala or white
  dessert wine
pinch of grated orange rind

1 In the top half of a double boiler, or in a heatproof bowl, away from the heat, whisk the egg yolks with the sugar until pale yellow.

2 Beat the Marsala or white dessert wine into the egg and sugar mixture.

3 Place the pan or bowl over a pan of simmering water and continue whisking for 6–8 minutes, or until the custard is a frothy, light mass and evenly coats the back of a spoon. Take care that you do not let the upper container touch the hot water, or the zabaglione may curdle.

4 Stir in the orange rind.

5 Spoon into individual dishes and serve immediately.

Variations
• Add a little ground cinnamon with the Marsala, if you like.
• Grated lemon rind or a drop of vanilla extract may be added for flavouring instead of orange rind.
• Substitute a mixture of 15ml/1 tbsp Kirsch, Chartreuse, brandy, rum or Kümmel and 60ml/4 tbsp white wine for the Marsala or dessert wine.

Tiramisu Energy 294Kcal/1231kJ; Protein 12.2g; Carbohydrate 27g, of which sugars 21.4g; Fat 14.3g, of which saturates 7.1g; Cholesterol 202mg; Calcium 43mg; Fibre 0.2g; Sodium 65mg.
Zabaglione Energy 108Kcal/452kJ; Protein 2.3g; Carbohydrate 12.9g, of which sugars 12.9g; Fat 4.1g, of which saturates 1.2g; Cholesterol 151mg; Calcium 26mg; Fibre 0g; Sodium 10mg.

Caribbean Chocolate Ring with Rum Syrup

This delectable dish brings you a taste of the Caribbean.

Serves 8–10
115g/4oz/½ cup unsalted (sweet) butter, plus extra for greasing
115g/4oz/scant ½ cup light muscovado (brown) sugar
2 eggs, beaten
2 ripe bananas, mashed
30ml/2 tbsp desiccated (dry unsweetened shredded) coconut
30ml/2 tbsp sour cream
115g/4oz/1 cup self-raising (self-rising) flour

45ml/3 tbsp cocoa powder (unsweetened)
2.5ml/½ tsp bicarbonate of soda (baking soda)

For the syrup
115g/4oz/generous ½ cup caster (superfine) sugar
60ml/4 tbsp water
30ml/2 tbsp dark rum
50g/2oz plain (semisweet) chocolate, chopped
mixture of tropical fruits and chocolate shapes or curls, to decorate

1 Preheat the oven to 180°C/350°F/Gas 4. Grease a 1.5 litre/2½ pint/6¼ cup ring tin (pan) with butter.

2 Cream the butter and sugar in a bowl until light and fluffy. Add the eggs gradually, beating well, then mix in the bananas, coconut and sour cream. Sift the flour, cocoa and bicarbonate of soda over the mixture and fold in thoroughly.

3 Transfer to the prepared tin and spread evenly. Bake for 45–50 minutes, until firm to the touch. Cool for 10 minutes in the tin, then turn out to finish cooling on a wire rack.

4 Make the syrup. Place the sugar in a small pan. Add the water and heat gently, stirring occasionally until dissolved. Bring to the boil and boil rapidly, without stirring, for 2 minutes. Remove from the heat.

5 Add the rum and chocolate to the syrup and stir until smooth, then spoon evenly over the top and sides of the cake. Decorate the ring with tropical fruits and chocolate shapes.

Old English Trifle

A wonderful combination of fruit, custard and cake laced with alcohol, this traditional English dessert is always popular.

Serves 6
75g/3oz day-old sponge cake, broken into bite-size pieces
8 ratafia biscuits (almond macaroons), broken into halves
100ml/3½fl oz/scant ½ cup medium sherry
30ml/2 tbsp brandy
350g/12oz prepared fruit such as raspberries, strawberries or peaches

300ml/½ pint/1¼ cups double (heavy) cream
40g/1½oz/⅓ cup toasted flaked (sliced) almonds
strawberries, to decorate

For the custard
4 egg yolks
25g/1oz/2 tbsp caster (superfine) sugar
450ml/¾ pint/scant 2 cups single (light) or whipping cream
few drops of vanilla extract

1 Put the sponge cake and ratafia biscuits in a glass serving dish, then sprinkle over the sherry and brandy and leave until the liquid has been absorbed.

2 Make the custard. Whisk the egg yolks and sugar together. Bring the cream to the boil in a heavy pan, then pour on to the egg yolk mixture, stirring constantly.

3 Return the mixture to the pan and heat very gently, stirring all the time with a wooden spoon, until the custard thickens enough to coat the back of the spoon; do not allow to boil. Leave to cool, stirring occasionally.

4 Arrange the fruit in an even layer over the soaked sponge cake in the serving dish, then strain the custard over the fruit and leave to set.

5 Lightly whip the cream, spread it over the custard, then chill the trifle well. Decorate with flaked almonds and strawberries just before serving.

Caribbean Choc. Ring Energy 315Kcal/1319kJ; Protein 4g; Carbohydrate 40.5g, of which sugars 31g; Fat 15.6g, of which saturates 9.7g; Cholesterol 65mg; Calcium 72mg; Fibre 1.6g; Sodium 172mg.
Trifle Energy 632Kcal/2616kJ; Protein 8.4g; Carbohydrate 24.9g, of which sugars 18.4g; Fat 53.1g, of which saturates 28.4g; Cholesterol 258mg; Calcium 155mg; Fibre 1.4g; Sodium 116mg.

Coconut Custard

This traditional dessert from South-east Asia can be baked or steamed and is often served with sweet sticky rice and a selection of fresh fruit. Mangoes and tamarillos go particularly well with the flavours.

Serves 4

4 eggs
75g/3oz/6 tbsp soft light brown
 sugar
250ml/8fl oz/1 cup coconut milk
5ml/1 tsp vanilla, rose or
 jasmine extract
fresh mint leaves and icing
 (confectioners') sugar,
 to decorate
sliced fruit, to serve

1 Preheat the oven to 150°C/300°F/Gas 2. Whisk the eggs and sugar in a bowl until smooth. Add the coconut milk and extract and whisk well.

2 Strain the mixture into a jug (pitcher), then pour it into four individual heatproof glasses or ramekins or an ovenproof dish.

3 Stand the glasses, ramekins or dish in a roasting pan. Fill the pan with hot water to reach halfway up the sides of the glasses, ramekins or dish.

4 Bake for about 35–40 minutes, or until the custards are set. Test with a fine skewer or cocktail stick (toothpick).

5 Remove the roasting pan from the oven, lift out the glasses, ramekins or dish and leave to cool.

6 If you like, turn out the custard(s) on to serving plate(s). Decorate with the mint leaves and a dusting of icing sugar, and serve with sliced fruit.

> **Cook's Tip**
> Before turning out the custard(s), first ease the edge of the custard away from the side of the dish with a sharp knife.

Zabaglione Ice Cream Torte

For anyone who likes zabaglione, the famous, whisked Italian dessert, this simple iced version is an absolute must! Its taste and texture are just as good, and there's no last-minute whisking to worry about.

Serves 10

175g/6oz amaretti
115g/4oz/½ cup ready-to-eat
 dried apricots, finely chopped

65g/2½oz/5 tbsp unsalted
 (sweet) butter, melted

For the ice cream
65g/2½oz/5 tbsp light
 muscovado (brown) sugar
75ml/5 tbsp water
5 egg yolks
250ml/8fl oz/1 cup
 double (heavy) cream
75ml/5 tbsp Madeira or cream
 sherry
poached fruit, to serve

1 Put the amaretti in a strong plastic bag and crush finely with a rolling pin. Turn into a bowl and stir in the apricots and melted butter until evenly combined.

2 Using a dampened spoon, pack the mixture on to the bottom and up the sides of a 24cm/9½in loose-based flan tin (tart pan) about 4cm/1½in deep. Chill.

3 Make the ice cream. Put the sugar and water in a small, heavy pan and heat, stirring, until the sugar has dissolved. Bring to the boil and boil for 2 minutes without stirring.

4 Whisk the egg yolks in a heatproof bowl until pale, then gradually whisk in the sugar syrup. Put the bowl over a pan of simmering water and continue to whisk for about 10 minutes or until the mixture leaves a trail when the whisk is lifted.

5 Remove from the heat and carry on whisking for a further 5 minutes or until the mixture is cold. In a separate bowl, whip the cream with the Madeira or sherry until it stands in peaks.

6 Using a large metal spoon, fold the cream into the whisked mixture. Spoon it into the lined tin, level the surface, cover and freeze overnight. Serve sliced, with a little poached fruit.

Coconut Custard Energy 161Kcal/681kJ; Protein 6.5g; Carbohydrate 22.7g, of which sugars 22.7g; Fat 5.7g, of which saturates 1.7g; Cholesterol 190mg; Calcium 57mg; Fibre 0g; Sodium 140mg.
Zabaglione Torte Energy 333Kcal/1387kJ; Protein 3.4g; Carbohydrate 25.8g, of which sugars 18.2g; Fat 23.9g, of which saturates 13.6g; Cholesterol 149mg; Calcium 60mg; Fibre 1g; Sodium 110mg.

French Chocolate Soufflés

These stylish French soufflés are actually extremely easy to make.

Serves 6

175g/6oz plain (semisweet) chocolate, chopped
150g/5oz/10 tbsp unsalted (sweet) butter, cut into small pieces
4 large (US extra large) eggs, separated
30ml/2 tbsp orange liqueur (optional)
1.5ml/¼ tsp cream of tartar
40g/1½oz/3 tbsp caster (superfine) sugar
icing (confectioners') sugar, for dusting
sprigs of redcurrants and white chocolate roses, to decorate

For the sauce

75g/3oz white chocolate, chopped
90ml/6 tbsp whipping cream
15–30ml/1–2 tbsp orange liqueur
grated rind of ½ orange

1 Generously butter six 150ml/¼ pint/⅔ cup ramekins, custard cups or small ovenproof dishes. Sprinkle each with a little sugar and tap out any excess. Place the dishes on a baking sheet.

2 Melt the chocolate and butter in a heavy pan over a very low heat, stirring until smooth. Remove from the heat and cool slightly, then beat in the egg yolks and orange liqueur, if using. Set aside, stirring occasionally.

3 Preheat the oven to 220°C/425°F/Gas 7. In a grease-free bowl, whisk the egg whites slowly until frothy. Add the cream of tartar, increase the speed and whisk to form soft peaks. Gradually whisk in the sugar until the whites are stiff and glossy. Stir a third of the whites into the cooled chocolate mixture, then fold this into the remaining whites. Spoon into the dishes.

4 Make the sauce. Put the white chocolate and cream in a small pan. Place over a low heat and cook, stirring constantly until smooth. Remove from the heat and stir in the liqueur and orange rind, then pour into a serving jug (pitcher); keep warm.

5 Bake the soufflés for 10–12 minutes until risen and set, but still slightly wobbly in the centre. Dust with icing sugar and decorate with redcurrants and chocolate roses. Serve with the sauce.

Crema Catalana

This fabulous Spanish dessert consists of a creamy custard topped with a net of brittle sugar – a Spanish variation on the theme of the crème brûlée. *Cremat* is the Catalan word for "burnt", and this was probably part of this dish's original name.

Serves 4

475ml/16fl oz/2 cups milk
pared rind of ½ lemon
1 cinnamon stick
4 large (US extra large) egg yolks
105ml/7 tbsp caster (superfine) sugar
25ml/1½ tbsp cornflour (cornstarch)
ground nutmeg, for sprinkling

1 Put the milk in a pan with the lemon rind and cinnamon stick. Bring to the boil, then simmer for 10 minutes. Remove the lemon rind and cinnamon. Put the egg yolks and 45ml/3 tbsp sugar in a bowl, and whisk until pale yellow. Add the cornflour and mix well.

2 Stir a few tablespoons of the hot milk into the egg yolk mixture, then pour back into the remaining milk. Return to the heat and cook gently, stirring, for about 5 minutes, until thickened and smooth. Do not boil.

3 Pour the custard into four shallow ovenproof dishes, measuring about 13cm/5in in diameter. Cool, then chill for a few hours, until firm.

4 No more than 30 minutes before you intend to serve the desserts, sprinkle the top of each one with 15ml/1 tbsp of the sugar and a little nutmeg.

5 Preheat the grill (broiler) to high. Place the dishes under the grill, on the highest shelf, and cook until the sugar caramelizes. This will take only a few seconds and they will caramelize unevenly, but this is normal. Do not leave them under the grill for too long in an attempt to make the effect even.

6 Leave the custards to cool for a few minutes before serving.

Chocolate Soufflés Energy 543Kcal/2256kJ; Protein 7.1g; Carbohydrate 35g, of which sugars 34.7g; Fat 42.3g, of which saturates 25g; Cholesterol 198mg; Calcium 80mg; Fibre 0.7g; Sodium 218mg.
Crema Catalana Energy 241Kcal/1020kJ; Protein 7.1g; Carbohydrate 38.8g, of which sugars 33g; Fat 7.6g, of which saturates 2.9g; Cholesterol 209mg; Calcium 181mg; Fibre 0g; Sodium 65mg.

Australian Hazelnut Pavlova

This dessert dish is created from meringue – enhanced with the added interest of hazelnuts – topped with a mixture of fresh fruits and cream. A delicious Australian speciality.

Serves 4–6
3 egg whites
175g/6oz/¾ cup caster
  (superfine) sugar
5ml/1 tsp cornflour (cornstarch)

5ml/1 tsp white wine vinegar
40g/1½oz/5 tbsp chopped
  roasted hazelnuts
250ml/8fl oz/1 cup double
  (heavy) cream
15ml/1 tbsp orange juice
30ml/2 tbsp natural (plain) thick
  and creamy yogurt
2 ripe nectarines, stoned
  (pitted) and sliced
225g/8oz/1⅓ cups raspberries
15–30ml/1–2 tbsp redcurrant
  jelly, warmed

1 Preheat the oven to 140°C/275°F/Gas 1. Lightly grease a baking sheet. Draw a 20cm/8in circle on a sheet of baking parchment. Place pencil-side down on the baking sheet.

2 Place the egg whites in a clean, grease-free bowl and whisk with an electric whisk until stiff.

3 Whisk in the sugar 15ml/1 tbsp at a time, whisking well after each addition.

4 Add the cornflour, vinegar and hazelnuts and fold in carefully with a large metal spoon.

5 Spoon the meringue on to the marked circle and spread out, making a dip in the centre.

6 Bake for about 1¼–1½ hours, until crisp. Leave to cool, then transfer to a serving platter.

7 Whip the cream and orange juice until just thick, stir in the yogurt and spoon on to the meringue.

8 Place the fruit on top of the cream and drizzle over the redcurrant jelly. Serve immediately.

Chocolate Fruit Fondue

Fondues originated in Switzerland and are best known as a way of enjoying various cheeses. However, the fondue is a very simple and tasty way of preparing all kinds of food and one that is ideally suited to sweet dishes. This particular version makes a fun dessert that also looks extremely attractive and appealing.

Serves 6–8
16 fresh strawberries
4 rings fresh pineapple,
  cut into wedges
2 small nectarines, stoned (pitted)

and cut into wedges
1 kiwi fruit, halved and
  thickly sliced
small bunch of black seedless
  grapes
2 bananas, chopped
1 small eating apple, cored and
  cut into wedges
lemon juice, for brushing
225g/8oz plain
  (semisweet) chocolate
15g/½oz/1 tbsp butter
150ml/¼ pint/⅔ cup single
  (light) cream
45ml/3 tbsp Irish cream
  liqueur
15ml/1 tbsp chopped pistachio
  nuts

1 Arrange the fruit on a serving platter and brush the banana and apple pieces with a little lemon juice. Cover and chill.

2 Place the chocolate, butter, cream and liqueur in a bowl over a pan of simmering water. Stir until smooth.

3 Pour into a warmed serving bowl and sprinkle with the pistachio nuts.

4 To eat, guests skewer the fruits on to forks, then dip them into the hot sauce.

Variations
Other delicious dippers for this fondue include cubes of sponge cake, sweet biscuits (cookies) such as amaretti, miniature marshmallows, ready-to-eat dried fruit, such as apricots, crêpes torn into pieces and popcorn.

Hazelnut Pavlova Energy 411Kcal/1715kJ; Protein 4.6g; Carbohydrate 40.3g, of which sugars 39.4g; Fat 26.8g, of which saturates 14.3g; Cholesterol 57mg; Calcium 69mg; Fibre 1.9g; Sodium 49mg.
Chocolate Fondue Energy 305Kcal/1282kJ; Protein 3.6g; Carbohydrate 39.7g, of which sugars 38.9g; Fat 15.2g, of which saturates 8.1g; Cholesterol 16mg; Calcium 51mg; Fibre 2.7g; Sodium 37mg.

Chilled Fruity Zucotto Sponge

An Italian-style dessert with a rich ricotta, fruit, chocolate and nut filling, zucotto is encased in a moist, chocolate and liqueur-flavoured sponge.

Serves 8

3 eggs
75g/3oz/6 tbsp caster
  (superfine) sugar
75g/3oz/⅔ cup plain
  (all-purpose) flour
25g/1oz/¼ cup cocoa powder
  (unsweetened)
90ml/6 tbsp Kirsch
250g/9oz/generous 1 cup
  ricotta cheese
50g/2oz/½ cup icing
  (confectioners') sugar
50g/2oz plain (semisweet)
  chocolate, finely chopped
50g/2oz/½ cup blanched
  almonds, chopped and toasted
75g/3oz/scant ½ cup natural
  glacé (candied) cherries,
  quartered
2 pieces preserved stem ginger,
  finely chopped
150ml/¼ pint/⅔ cup double
  (heavy) cream
cocoa powder (unsweetened), for
  dusting

1 Preheat the oven to 180°C/350°F/Gas 4. Grease and line a 23cm/9in cake tin (pan). Whisk the eggs and sugar in a heatproof bowl over a pan of simmering water until the whisk leaves a trail. Remove the bowl from the heat and continue to whisk the mixture for 2 minutes.

2 Sift the flour and cocoa into the bowl and fold it in with a large metal spoon. Spoon the mixture into the prepared tin and bake for about 20 minutes until just firm. Leave to cool.

3 Cut the cake horizontally into three layers. Set aside 30ml/2 tbsp of the Kirsch. Drizzle the remaining Kirsch over the layers.

4 Beat the ricotta cheese in a bowl until softened, then beat in the icing sugar, chopped chocolate, toasted almonds, cherries, stem ginger and reserved Kirsch.

5 Pour the cream into a separate bowl and whip it lightly. Using a large metal spoon, fold the cream into the ricotta mixture. Chill. Cut a 20cm/8in circle from one sponge layer, using a plate as a guide, and set it aside.

6 Use the remaining sponge to make the case for the zucotto. Cut the cake to fit the bottom of a 2.8–3.4 litre/5–6 pint/12½–15 cup freezerproof mixing bowl. Cut more sponge for the sides of the bowl, fitting the pieces together and taking them about one-third of the way up.

7 Spoon the ricotta filling into the bowl up to the height of the sponge, and level the surface.

8 Fit the reserved circle of sponge on top of the filling. Trim off the excess sponge around the edges. Cover the bowl and freeze overnight.

9 Transfer the zucotto to the refrigerator 45 minutes before serving, so that the filling softens slightly. Invert it on to a serving plate and peel away the clear film (plastic wrap). Dust with cocoa powder and serve immediately in slices.

Coconut Rice with Fruit Coulis

Desserts similar to this coconut treat are served in countries all over the Far East, often accompanied by fresh tropical fruit, such as mangoes, pineapple and guavas.

Serves 4–6

75g/3oz/scant ½ cup jasmine
  rice, soaked overnight in
  175ml/6fl oz/¾ cup water
350ml/12fl oz/1½ cups
  coconut milk
150ml/¼ pint/⅔ cup single
  (light) cream
50g/2oz/¼ cup caster
  (superfine) sugar
raspberries and fresh mint leaves,
  to decorate

For the coulis
75g/3oz/¾ cup blackcurrants,
  stalks removed
25g/1oz/2 tbsp caster
  (superfine) sugar
75g/3oz/½ cup fresh or
  frozen raspberries

1 Put the rice and its soaking water into a food processor and process for a few minutes until the mixture is soupy.

2 Heat the coconut milk and cream in a non-stick pan. When the mixture is on the point of boiling, stir in the rice mixture. Cook over a very gentle heat for 10 minutes, stirring constantly.

3 Stir the sugar into the coconut rice mixture and continue cooking for a further 10–15 minutes, or until thick and creamy.

4 Line a rectangular tin (pan) with non-stick baking parchment. Pour the coconut rice mixture into the pan, cool, then chill in the refrigerator until the dessert is set and firm.

5 Meanwhile, make the coulis. Put the blackcurrants in a bowl and sprinkle with the sugar. Set aside for 30 minutes. Turn the blackcurrants and raspberries into a sieve (strainer) set over a bowl. Using a spoon, press the fruit so that the juices collect in the bowl. Taste the coulis and add more sugar if necessary.

6 Cut the coconut cream into diamonds. Spoon a little coulis on to individual plates, arrange the diamonds on top and decorate with raspberries and mint leaves. Serve immediately.

Zucotto Sponge Energy 391Kcal/1631kJ; Protein 8.7g; Carbohydrate 33.8g, of which sugars 26.1g; Fat 22.7g, of which saturates 11.4g; Cholesterol 111mg; Calcium 66mg; Fibre 1.4g; Sodium 64mg.
Coconut Rice Energy 165Kcal/696kJ; Protein 2.3g; Carbohydrate 28.7g, of which sugars 18.8g; Fat 5.1g, of which saturates 3.2g; Cholesterol 14mg; Calcium 59mg; Fibre 0.8g; Sodium 73mg.

Classic Crème Brûlée

This dessert actually originated in Cambridge, England, but has become associated with France and is widely eaten there. Add a little liqueur, if you like, but it is equally delicious without it.

Serves 6
1 vanilla pod (bean)
1 litre/1¾ pints/4 cups double (heavy) cream
6 egg yolks
90g/3½oz/½ cup caster (superfine) sugar
30ml/2 tbsp almond or orange liqueur (optional)
75g/3oz/6 tbsp soft light brown sugar

1 Preheat the oven to 150°C/300°F/Gas 2. Place six 120ml/ 4fl oz/½ cup ramekins, custard cups or small ovenproof dishes in a roasting pan and set aside.

2 With a small sharp knife, split the vanilla pod lengthways and scrape the black seeds into a medium pan. Add the cream and bring just to the boil over a medium heat, stirring. Remove from the heat and cover. Set aside for 15–20 minutes.

3 In a bowl, whisk the egg yolks, caster sugar and liqueur, if using, until well blended. Whisk in the hot cream and strain into a large jug (pitcher). Divide the custard among the dishes.

4 Pour enough boiling water into the roasting pan to come halfway up the sides of the dishes. Cover the pan with foil and bake for about 30 minutes until the custards are just set. Remove from the pan and leave to cool. Return to the dry roasting pan and chill.

5 Preheat the grill (broiler). Sprinkle the sugar evenly over the surface of each custard and grill (broil) for 30–60 seconds until the sugar melts and caramelizes. Do not let the sugar burn or allow the custard to curdle.

6 Place in the refrigerator to set the crust and chill completely before serving.

Crème Caramel

One of the most popular French desserts, this is a slightly lighter version of the traditional recipe.

Serves 6–8
250g/9oz/1¼ cups granulated sugar
60ml/4 tbsp water

1 vanilla pod (bean) or 10ml/ 2 tsp vanilla extract
400ml/14fl oz/1⅔ cups milk
250ml/8fl oz/1 cup whipping cream
5 large (US extra large) eggs
2 egg yolks

1 Put 175g/6oz/¾ cup of the sugar in a small heavy pan with the water to moisten. Bring to the boil over a high heat, swirling the pan to dissolve the sugar. Boil, without stirring, for 4–5 minutes until the syrup turns a dark caramel colour.

2 Immediately pour the caramel into a 1 litre/1¾ pint/4 cup soufflé dish. Holding the dish with oven gloves, quickly swirl the dish to coat the base and sides with the caramel and set aside. (The caramel will harden quickly.) Place in a roasting pan.

3 Preheat the oven to 160°C/325°F/Gas 3. With a knife, split the vanilla pod lengthways and scrape the black seeds into a medium pan. Add the milk and cream and bring just to the boil over a medium-high heat, stirring frequently. Remove the pan from the heat, cover and set aside for 15–20 minutes.

4 In a bowl, whisk the eggs and egg yolks with the remaining sugar for 2–3 minutes until creamy. Whisk in the hot milk and carefully strain the mixture into the lined dish. Cover with foil.

5 Pour enough boiling water into the roasting pan to come halfway up the sides of the filled dish. Bake the custard for 40–45 minutes until just set. Remove from the roasting pan and cool for at least 30 minutes, then chill overnight.

6 Run a sharp knife around the edge of the dish, cover with a serving plate, hold together tightly and invert. Lift one edge of the dish, allowing the caramel to run out, then remove the dish.

Crème Brûlée Energy 996Kcal/4116kJ; Protein 5.7g; Carbohydrate 31.6g, of which sugars 31.6g; Fat 95g, of which saturates 57.2g; Cholesterol 430mg; Calcium 120mg; Fibre 0g; Sodium 47mg.
Crème Caramel Energy 326Kcal/1367kJ; Protein 7.1g; Carbohydrate 35.9g, of which sugars 35.9g; Fat 18.3g, of which saturates 9.8g; Cholesterol 205mg; Calcium 118mg; Fibre 0g; Sodium 77mg.

French Floating Islands

Bring a touch of French elegance to the table with delicate meringues floating on a vanilla custard.

Serves 4–6
1 vanilla pod (bean)
600ml/1 pint/2½ cups milk
8 egg yolks
50g/2oz/¼ cup granulated sugar

For the meringues
4 large (US extra large)
   egg whites
1.5ml/¼ tsp cream of tartar
225g/8oz/1 cup caster
   (superfine) sugar

For the caramel
150g/5oz/¾ cup granulated
   sugar
45ml/3 tbsp water

1 Split the vanilla pod lengthways and scrape the seeds into a pan. Add the milk and bring just to the boil over a medium heat, stirring frequently. Cover and set aside for 15–20 minutes.

2 In a medium bowl, whisk the egg yolks and sugar for 2–3 minutes until thick and creamy. Whisk in the hot milk and return the mixture to the pan. With a wooden spoon, stir over a medium-low heat until the sauce begins to thicken and coat the back of the spoon (do not allow to boil). Immediately strain into a chilled bowl, allow to cool, stirring occasionally and then chill.

3 Half-fill a large wide pan with water and bring just to simmering point. In a grease-free bowl, whisk the egg whites until frothy. Add the cream of tartar and continue whisking to form soft peaks. Gradually whisk in the sugar, until stiff and glossy.

4 Using two tablespoons, form egg-shaped meringues and poach for 2–3 minutes, turning once until just firm. Using a slotted spoon, transfer the meringues to a baking sheet lined with kitchen paper to drain.

5 Pour the cold custard into individual serving dishes and arrange the meringues on top. Put the sugar into a small pan with the water. Boil, without stirring, until the syrup turns a dark caramel colour. Immediately drizzle the caramel over the meringues and custard. Serve cold.

Peach Melba

The story goes that the great French chef, Auguste Escoffier, created this dessert in honour of the opera singer Nellie Melba.

Serves 6
50g/2oz/¼ cup caster
   (superfine) sugar
1 litre/1¾ pints/4 cups water
1 vanilla pod (bean), split
3 large peaches

For the sauce
450g/1lb/2⅔ cups fresh or frozen
   raspberries
15ml/1 tbsp lemon juice
25–40g/1–1½oz/2–3 tbsp caster
   (superfine) sugar
30–45ml/2–3 tbsp raspberry
   liqueur (optional)
vanilla ice cream, to serve
mint leaves and fresh raspberries,
   to decorate

1 Put the sugar, water and vanilla pod in a pan large enough to hold the peach halves in a single layer. Bring to the boil, over a medium heat, stirring occasionally to dissolve the sugar.

2 Cut the peaches in half and remove the peach stones (pits). Add the peach halves to the syrup, cut-sides down, adding more water, if needed, to cover the fruit. Press a piece of baking parchment against the surface, reduce the heat to medium-low, then cover and simmer for 12–15 minutes until tender – the time will depend on the ripeness of the fruit. Remove the pan from the heat and leave the peaches to cool in the syrup.

3 Remove the peaches from the syrup and peel off the skins. Place on several thicknesses of kitchen paper to drain (reserve the syrup for another use), then cover and chill.

4 Put the raspberries, lemon juice and sugar in a blender or food processor fitted with the metal blade. Process for 1 minute, scraping down the sides once. Press through a fine sieve (strainer) into a small bowl, then stir in the raspberry liqueur, if using, and put in the refrigerator to chill.

5 To serve, place a peach half, cut-side up, on a plate, fill with a scoop of ice cream and spoon the raspberry sauce over the top. Decorate with mint and a few fresh raspberries.

Floating Islands Energy 414Kcal/1755kJ; Protein 9.5g; Carbohydrate 78.7g, of which sugars 78.7g; Fat 9g, of which saturates 3.2g; Cholesterol 275mg; Calcium 190mg; Fibre 0g; Sodium 100mg.
Peach Melba Energy 93Kcal/398kJ; Protein 1.9g; Carbohydrate 22.2g, of which sugars 22.2g; Fat 0.3g, of which saturates 0.1g; Cholesterol 0mg; Calcium 31mg; Fibre 3g; Sodium 4mg.

Apple-Stuffed Crêpes

Spain's dairy country lies along the cooler northern coast and crêpes are extremely popular there. The Asturias, which run east to west along the coast, are apple and cider country, too, and crêpes, which are known as *frisuelos*, are made with a variety of sweet fillings, such as this succulent apple one.

Serves 4
115g/4oz/1 cup plain
 (all-purpose) flour
pinch of salt
2 large (US extra large) eggs
175ml/6fl oz/³⁄4 cup milk
120ml/4fl oz/¹⁄2 cup sweet
 (hard) cider
butter, for frying
4 eating apples
50g/2oz/¹⁄4 cup caster (superfine)
 sugar
120ml/8 tbsp clear honey
150ml/¹⁄4 pint/²⁄3 cup double
 (heavy) cream, to serve

1 Make the batter. Sift the flour and salt into a large bowl. Add the eggs and milk and beat until smooth. Stir in the cider. Leave to stand for 30 minutes.

2 Heat a small heavy non-stick frying pan. Add a little butter and ladle in enough batter to coat the pan thinly.

3 Cook the crêpe for about 1 minute until it is golden underneath, then flip it over and cook the other side until golden. Slide the crêpe on to a plate, then repeat with the remaining batter to make seven more. Set the crêpes aside and keep warm.

4 Make the apple filling. Cut the apples into quarters and remove the cores, then cut them into thick slices. Heat 15g/¹⁄2oz butter in a large frying pan. Add the apples to the pan and cook until golden on both sides. Transfer the slices to a bowl with a slotted spoon and sprinkle with sugar.

5 Fold each pancake in half, then fold in half again to form a cone. Fill each with some of the fried apples. Place two filled pancakes on each dessert plate. Drizzle each with 15ml/1 tbsp honey and serve at once, accompanied by cream.

Crêpes Suzette

These classic French crêpes are an absolute winner.

Serves 4
115g/4oz/1 cup plain
 (all-purpose) flour
1 egg
1 egg yolk
300ml/¹⁄2 pint/1¹⁄4 cups
 skimmed milk
15g/¹⁄2oz/1 tbsp unsalted (sweet)
butter, melted, plus extra butter
for frying

For the sauce
25g/1oz/2 tbsp unsalted (sweet)
 butter
50g/2oz/¹⁄4 cup caster (superfine)
 sugar
juice of 2 oranges
juice of ¹⁄2 lemon
60ml/4 tbsp orange liqueur

1 Sift the flour into a bowl and make a well in the centre. Add the egg and the extra yolk to the well. Stir with a wooden spoon to incorporate the flour from around the edges. Gradually beat in the milk to form a smooth batter. Stir in the melted butter, transfer to a measuring jug (cup) and chill.

2 Heat a 20cm/8in shallow frying pan, add a little butter and heat until sizzling. Pour in a little of the batter, tilting the pan to cover the base thinly.

3 Cook the crêpes over a medium heat for 1–2 minutes until lightly browned underneath, then flip over and cook for 1 minute. Repeat this process until you have eight crêpes.

4 Make the sauce. Melt the butter in a heavy frying pan. Stir in the caster sugar and cook over a medium heat, tilting the pan occasionally, until the mixture is golden brown. Add the orange and lemon juices and stir until the caramel has dissolved.

5 Add a crêpe to the pan. Using kitchen tongs, fold it in half, then in half again. Slide to the side of the pan. Repeat with the remaining crêpes.

6 When all the crêpes have been folded in the sauce, pour over the liqueur and set it alight. Shake the pan until the flames die down. Divide the crêpes and sauce among individual plates.

Crêpes Suzette Energy 336Kcal/1410kJ; Protein 7.8g; Carbohydrate 44.6g, of which sugars 22.7g; Fat 11.6g, of which saturates 6.2g; Cholesterol 122mg; Calcium 156mg; Fibre 0.9g; Sodium 118mg.
Apple-Stuffed Crêpes Energy 411Kcal/1736kJ; Protein 7.8g; Carbohydrate 70.3g, of which sugars 48.4g; Fat 12.2g, of which saturates 6.5g; Cholesterol 119mg; Calcium 123mg; Fibre 2g; Sodium 123mg.

Middle Eastern Pestiños

The Arabs invented sweet bites like these to eat after the main course.

Makes about 30
225g/8oz/2 cups plain (all-purpose) flour, plus extra for dusting
60ml/4 tbsp sunflower oil
15ml/1 tbsp aniseed, lightly crushed
40g/1½oz/3 tbsp caster (superfine) sugar
250ml/8fl oz/1 cup water
60ml/4 tbsp anisette or other anis spirit, such as Ricard
3 small (US medium) eggs

For the anis syrup
60ml/4 tbsp clear honey
60ml/4 tbsp anisette or other anis spirit, such as Ricard

1 Preheat the oven to 190°C/375°F/Gas 5. Sift the flour on to a sheet of baking parchment. Heat the oil in a small pan with the crushed aniseed, until the aniseed releases its aroma. Strain the oil into a larger pan and add the sugar, water and anisette. Heat to a rolling boil.

2 Remove the pan from the heat and add the sifted flour, all in one go. Beat vigorously with a wooden spoon until the mixture leaves the sides of the pan clean. Leave to cool.

3 Meanwhile lightly beat the eggs. Gradually incorporate the egg into the dough mixture, beating hard. You may not need to use all the egg – the paste should be soft but not sloppy. Reserve any remaining beaten egg.

4 Grease and flour two baking sheets. Fit a plain nozzle to a piping (pastry) bag and pipe small rounds of dough about 2.5cm/1in across on the sheets, spacing them about 2.5cm/1in apart. Brush with the remaining beaten egg.

5 Bake for about 30 minutes, or until lightly brown and an even texture all the way through. (Lift one off the sheet to test.)

6 Make the syrup. Melt the honey in a small pan and stir in the anisette. Just before serving, use a slotted spoon to dunk the pestiños into the syrup.

Chocolate Profiteroles

This mouth-watering dessert is served in cafés throughout France. Sometimes the profiteroles are filled with whipped cream instead of ice cream.

Serves 4–6
275g/10oz plain (semisweet) chocolate
120ml/4fl oz/½ cup warm water
750ml/1¼ pints/3 cups vanilla ice cream

For the profiteroles
110g/3¾oz/scant 1 cup plain (all-purpose) flour
1.5ml/¼ tsp salt
pinch of freshly grated nutmeg
75g/3oz/6 tbsp unsalted (sweet) butter, cut into 6 pieces, plus extra for greasing
175ml/6fl oz/¾ cup water
3 eggs

1 Preheat the oven to 200°C/400°F/Gas 6 and butter a baking sheet.

2 Make the profiteroles. Sift together the flour, salt and nutmeg. In a medium pan, bring the butter and the water to the boil. Remove from the heat and add the dry ingredients all at once. Beat with a wooden spoon for about 1 minute until blended and the mixture starts to pull away from the sides of the pan, then set the pan over a low heat and cook the mixture for about 2 minutes, beating constantly. Remove from the heat.

3 Beat one egg in a small bowl and set aside. Add the remaining eggs, one at a time, to the flour mixture, beating well. Add the beaten egg gradually until the dough is smooth and shiny; it should fall slowly when dropped from a spoon.

4 Using a tablespoon, drop the dough on to the baking sheet in 12 mounds. Bake for 25–30 minutes until the pastry is well risen and browned. Turn off the oven and leave the puffs to cool with the oven door open.

5 Melt the chocolate and warm water in a bowl over a pan of hot water. Split the profiteroles in half and put a small scoop of ice cream in each. Pour the sauce over the top and serve.

Pestiños Energy 70Kcal/296kJ; Protein 1.3g; Carbohydrate 9.9g, of which sugars 4.2g; Fat 2.1g, of which saturates 0.3g; Cholesterol 19mg; Calcium 14mg; Fibre 0.2g; Sodium 8mg.
Profiteroles Energy 647Kcal/2707kJ; Protein 11.7g; Carbohydrate 68.2g, of which sugars 52.4g; Fat 36.9g, of which saturates 22.7g; Cholesterol 155mg; Calcium 182mg; Fibre 1.7g; Sodium 189mg.

Coconut Dumplings with Apricot Sauce

Based on a simple Asian recipe, these delicate little dumplings are very quick to cook. The sharp flavour of the sauce offsets the creamy dumplings beautifully.

Serves 4
75g/3oz/6 tbsp low-fat cottage cheese
1 egg white
15ml/1 tbsp low-fat spread
15ml/1 tbsp light muscovado (brown) sugar

30ml/2 tbsp self-raising (self-rising) wholemeal (whole-wheat) flour
finely grated rind of ½ lemon
15ml/1 tbsp desiccated (dry unsweetened shredded) coconut, toasted

For the sauce
225g/8oz can apricot halves in natural juice
15ml/1 tbsp lemon juice

1 Half-fill a steamer with boiling water and put it on to boil. If you do not own a steamer, place a heatproof plate over a pan of boiling water.

2 Beat together the cottage cheese, egg white and low-fat spread until they are evenly mixed.

3 Stir in the sugar, flour, lemon rind and coconut, mixing everything evenly to a fairly firm dough.

4 Place 8–12 spoonfuls of the mixture in the steamer or on the plate, leaving a space between them.

5 Cover the steamer or pan tightly with a lid or a plate and steam for about 10 minutes, until the dumplings have risen and are firm to the touch.

6 Make the sauce in a mixing bowl. Purée the can of apricots and stir in the lemon juice. Pour into a small pan and heat until boiling, then serve with the dumplings. Sprinkle with extra coconut to serve.

Peach & Ginger Pashka

A low-fat version of the Russian Easter favourite – a glorious cheese dessert flavoured with peaches and preserved stem ginger.

Serves 4
350g/12oz/1½ cups low-fat cottage cheese
2 ripe peaches or nectarines
90g/3½oz/scant ½ cup low-fat natural (plain) yogurt

2 pieces preserved stem ginger in syrup, drained and chopped, plus 30ml/2 tbsp syrup from the jar
2.5ml/½ tsp vanilla extract

To decorate
1 peach or nectarine, peeled and sliced
10ml/2 tsp slivered almonds, toasted

1 Drain the cottage cheese and rub it through a fine sieve (strainer) into a bowl. Remove the stones (pits) from the peaches or nectarines and roughly chop.

2 Mix together the chopped peaches or nectarines in a large bowl with the low-fat cottage cheese, yogurt, preserved stem ginger, syrup and vanilla extract.

3 Line a new, clean flower pot or a sieve (strainer) with a piece of clean, fine cloth, such as muslin (cheesecloth).

4 Add the cheese mixture and wrap over the cloth to cover. Place a saucer on top and weigh down. Stand over a bowl in a cool place and leave to drain overnight.

5 To serve, unwrap the cloth and turn the pashka out on to a serving plate. Decorate the pashka with peach or nectarine slices and toasted almonds.

Cook's Tip
Rather than making one large pashka, line four to six cups or ramekins with the clean cloth or muslin (cheesecloth) and divide the mixture evenly among them.

Coconut Dumplings Energy 134Kcal/565kJ; Protein 4.4g; Carbohydrate 19.5g, of which sugars 13.9g; Fat 4.7g, of which saturates 2.9g; Cholesterol 3mg; Calcium 66mg; Fibre 1.3g; Sodium 130mg.
Pashka Energy 157Kcal/660kJ; Protein 13.3g; Carbohydrate 14.7g, of which sugars 14.6g; Fat 5.1g, of which saturates 2.3g; Cholesterol 14mg; Calcium 165mg; Fibre 1g; Sodium 302mg.

Lemon Tartlets

These classic French tartlets make a most delicious dessert. A luscious lemon curd is encased in rich pastry and decorated with caramelized lemon slices.

Makes 12
6 eggs, beaten
350g/12oz/1½ cups caster (superfine) sugar
115g/4oz/½ cup butter
grated rind and juice of 4 lemons
icing (confectioners') sugar, for dusting (optional)
175ml/6fl oz/¾ cup double (heavy) cream, to serve

For the pastry
225g/8oz/2 cups plain (all-purpose) flour
115g/4oz/½ cup chilled butter, diced
30ml/2 tbsp icing (confectioners') sugar
1 egg, beaten
5ml/1 tsp vanilla extract
15ml/1 tbsp chilled water

For the topping
2 lemons, well scrubbed
75ml/5 tbsp apricot jam

1 Preheat the oven to 200°C/100°F/Gas 6. Make the pastry. Sift the flour into a large mixing bowl. Using your fingertips, lightly rub the butter into the flour until the mixture resembles fine breadcrumbs. Add the icing sugar and stir well to mix.

2 Add the egg, vanilla extract and most of the chilled water, then work to a soft dough. Add a few more drops of water if necessary. Knead quickly and lightly, while still in the bowl, until a smooth dough forms.

3 Lightly butter twelve 10cm/4in tartlet tins (muffin pans). Roll out the pastry on a lightly floured work surface to a thickness of 3mm/⅛in.

4 Using a 10cm/4in fluted pastry (cookie) cutter, cut out 12 rounds and press them into the tartlet tins. Prick the bases all over with a fork and then transfer the tins to a baking sheet.

5 Line the pastry cases (pie shells) with baking parchment and fill with baking beans. Bake the pastry cases for 10 minutes. Remove the paper and beans. Set the tins aside while you make the filling.

6 Put the eggs, sugar and butter in a pan, and stir over a low heat until all the sugar has dissolved. Add the lemon rind and juice, and continue cooking, stirring constantly, until the lemon curd has thickened slightly.

7 Pour the lemon curd mixture into the pastry cases. Bake for 15 minutes, or until the curd filling is almost set.

8 Prepare the topping while the lemon tartlets are cooking. Cut the lemons into 12 slices, then cut the slices in half.

9 Push the jam through a fine sieve (strainer), then transfer to a small pan and heat. Place two lemon slices in the centre of each tartlet, overlapping them if you wish. Lightly brush the top of the tartlet with the strained jam, then put under the grill (broiler) and heat for 5 minutes, or until the top is caramelized and golden. Serve with cream.

Mexican Sopaipillas

These golden pillows of fried pastry from Mexico can be served as a dessert with honey or plain with soups.

Makes about 30
225g/8oz/2 cups plain (all-purpose) flour
15ml/1 tsp baking powder

5ml/1 tsp salt
25g/1oz/2 tbsp white cooking fat or margarine
175ml/6fl oz/¾ cup warm water
oil, for deep frying
clear honey, for drizzling
ground cinnamon, for sprinkling
crème fraîche or thick double (heavy) cream, to serve

1 Sift the flour, baking powder and salt into a mixing bowl. Rub in the cooking fat or margarine until the mixture resembles fine breadcrumbs. Gradually add enough of the water to form a dough. Wrap the dough in clear film (plastic wrap) and leave for 1 hour.

2 Working with half the dough at a time, roll it out to a square, keeping it as even and as thin as possible. Cut into 7.5cm/3in squares. When both pieces of the dough have been rolled and cut, set the squares aside.

3 Heat the oil for deep frying to 190°C/375°F, or until a cube of dried bread added to the oil floats and turns golden after 1 minute. Add a few pastry squares, using tongs to push them down into the oil. Cook in batches until golden on both sides, turning them once, and drain on kitchen paper.

4 When all the sopaipillas have been cooked, arrange them on a large serving plate, drizzle with honey and sprinkle lightly with ground cinnamon. Serve warm, with dollops of crème fraîche or thick double cream.

Variation
Instead of drizzling honey over the sopaipillas, try using a mixture of 50g/2oz/¼ cup caster (superfine) sugar and 10ml/2 tsp ground cinnamon.

Lemon Tartlets Energy 391Kcal/1639kJ; Protein 5.7g; Carbohydrate 52.1g, of which sugars 37.8g; Fat 19.2g, of which saturates 10.9g; Cholesterol 152mg; Calcium 64mg; Fibre 0.6g; Sodium 162mg.
Sopaipillas Energy 107Kcal/442kJ; Protein 0.7g; Carbohydrate 5.8g, of which sugars 0.1g; Fat 9.1g, of which saturates 1.1g; Cholesterol 0mg; Calcium 11mg; Fibre 0.2g; Sodium 72mg.

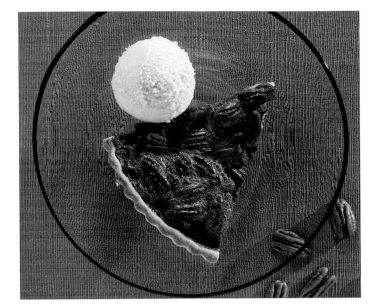

Mississippi Pecan Pie

This fabulous dessert started life in the United States but has become an international favourite.

Serves 6–8
115g/4oz/1 cup plain
   (all-purpose) flour
50g/2oz/4 tbsp butter, cubed
25g/1oz/2 tbsp caster
   (superfine) sugar
1 egg yolk
30ml/2 tbsp water

For the filling
175g/6oz/1/2 cup golden (light
   corn) syrup
50g/2oz/1/4 cup dark muscovado
   (molasses) sugar
50g/2oz/4 tbsp butter
3 eggs, lightly beaten
2.5ml/1/2 tsp vanilla extract
150g/5oz/11/4 cups pecan nuts
fresh cream or ice cream, to serve

1 Place the flour in a bowl and add the butter. Rub in the butter with your fingertips until the mixture resembles breadcrumbs, then stir in the sugar, egg yolk and the water. Mix to a dough and knead lightly on a floured surface until smooth.

2 Roll out the pastry and use to line a 20cm/8in loose-based fluted flan tin (tart pan). Prick the base, then line with baking parchment and fill with baking beans. Chill for 30 minutes. Preheat the oven to 200°C/400°F/Gas 6.

3 Bake the pastry case (pie shell) for 10 minutes. Remove the paper and beans and bake for a further 5 minutes. Reduce the oven temperature to 180°C/350°F/Gas 4.

4 Meanwhile, heat the syrup, sugar and butter in a pan until the sugar dissolves. Remove from the heat and cool slightly. Whisk in the eggs and vanilla extract and stir in the pecans. Pour into the pastry case and bake for 35–40 minutes, until the filling is set. Serve with cream or ice cream.

> **Cook's Tip**
> *Cooking the pastry before filling stops it from turning soggy.*

Key Lime Pie

This American dish hails from the Florida Keys.

Makes 10 slices
225g/8oz/2 cups plain
   (all-purpose) flour
115g/4oz/1/2 cup chilled
   butter, diced
25g/1oz/2 tbsp caster
   (superfine) sugar
2 egg yolks
pinch of salt
30ml/2 tbsp cold water
shredded, thinly pared lime rind
   and mint leaves, to decorate

For the filling
4 eggs, separated
400g/14oz can condensed milk
grated rind and juice of 3 limes
a few drops of green food
   colouring (optional)
25g/1oz/2 tbsp caster
   (superfine) sugar

For the topping
300ml/1/2 pint/11/4 cups double
   (heavy) cream
2 or 3 limes, thinly sliced

1 Sift the flour into a bowl and rub in the butter until the mixture resembles breadcrumbs. Add the sugar, egg yolks, salt and water. Mix to a soft dough. Roll out the pastry on a lightly floured surface and use to line a deep 21cm/81/2in fluted flan tin (tart pan), letting excess pastry hang over the edge. Prick the pastry base. Chill for 30 minutes. Preheat the oven to 200°C/400°F/Gas 6. Trim off the excess pastry and line the pastry case (pie shell) with parchment and baking beans. Bake blind for 10 minutes. Remove the paper and beans and return the pastry case to the oven for 10 minutes.

2 Meanwhile, make the filling. Beat the egg yolks in a bowl until light and creamy, then beat in the condensed milk, lime rind and juice. Add the food colouring, if using, and beat until the mixture is thick. In a grease-free bowl, whisk the egg whites to stiff peaks. Whisk in the caster sugar, then fold into the lime mixture.

3 Lower the oven to 160°C/325°F/Gas 3. Pour the filling into the pastry case. Bake for 20–25 minutes, until it has set and starts to brown. Cool, then chill. Before serving, whip the cream and spoon it around the edge of the pie. Cut the lime slices once from the centre to the edge, twist each one and arrange on the cream. Decorate with lime rind and mint.

Pecan Pie Energy 409Kcal/1705kJ; Protein 6g; Carbohydrate 39.4g, of which sugars 28.2g; Fat 26.4g, of which saturates 8.4g; Cholesterol 123mg; Calcium 56mg; Fibre 1.3g; Sodium 163mg.
Key Lime Pie Energy 510Kcal/2126kJ; Protein 9.2g; Carbohydrate 46.6g, of which sugars 29.4g; Fat 33.2g, of which saturates 19.5g; Cholesterol 196mg; Calcium 182mg; Fibre 0.7g; Sodium 163mg.

Apple Pie

An English and American classic, delicious on its own or with a dollop of cream.

1.5ml/¼ tsp grated nutmeg
1.5ml/¼ tsp salt
50g/2oz/4 tbsp butter, diced

Serves 8
900g/2lb tart cooking apples
25g/1oz/¼ cup plain
  (all-purpose) flour
90g/3½oz/½ cup sugar
25ml/1½ tbsp fresh lemon juice
2.5ml/½ tsp ground cinnamon
2.5ml/½ tsp ground allspice
1.5ml/¼ tsp ground ginger

For the pastry
225g/8oz/2 cups plain
  (all-purpose) flour
5ml/1 tsp salt
75g/3oz/6 tbsp cold butter, cut
  into pieces
50g/2oz/4 tbsp cold lard, cut
  into pieces
60–120ml/4–8 tbsp iced water

1 Make the pastry. Sift the flour and salt into a bowl. Add the butter and lard and cut in with a pastry blender or rub with your fingertips until the mixture resembles coarse breadcrumbs. Stir in just enough iced water to bind the dough. Form into two balls, wrap in clear film (plastic wrap) and chill for 20 minutes.

2 On a lightly floured surface, roll out one dough ball to 3mm/⅛in thick. Transfer to a 23cm/9in pie tin (pan) and trim the edge. Place a baking sheet in the centre of the oven and preheat to 220°C/425°F/Gas 7.

3 Peel, core and slice the apples into a bowl. Toss with the flour, sugar, lemon juice, spices and salt. Spoon into the pastry case (pie shell) and dot with butter.

4 Roll out the remaining dough. Place on top of the pie and trim to leave a 2cm/¾in overhang. Fold the overhang under the bottom dough and press to seal. Crimp the edge. Roll out the leftover pastry and cut out leaf shapes and roll balls. Arrange on top of the pie. Cut steam vents.

5 Bake for 10 minutes. Reduce the heat to 180°C/350°F/Gas 4 and bake for 40–45 minutes more until golden. If the pie browns too quickly, protect the top with foil.

Apple & Orange Pie

Oranges add an evocative Mediterranean twist to an Anglo-American favourite.

Serves 4–6
3 navel oranges
1kg/2¼lb cooking apples, peeled, cored and thickly sliced
30ml/2 tbsp demerara
  (raw) sugar
beaten egg, to glaze

caster (superfine) sugar,
  for sprinkling

For the pastry
275g/10oz/2½ cups plain
  (all-purpose) flour
2.5ml/½ tsp salt
150g/5oz/10 tbsp chilled
  butter, diced
about 45ml/4 tbsp chilled
  water

1 Make the pastry. Sift the flour and salt into a large bowl. Rub in the butter with your fingertips, until the mixture resembles fine breadcrumbs. Mix in the water and knead lightly to form a firm dough. Wrap the dough in clear film (plastic wrap) and chill for at least 30 minutes.

2 Roll out the pastry on a lightly floured work surface to a shape 2cm/¾in larger than the top of a 1.2 litre/2 pint/5 cup pie dish. Cut off a narrow strip around the edge of the pastry, brush it with a little cold water and firmly attach it to the rim of the pie dish.

3 Preheat the oven to 190°C/375°F/Gas 5. Using a sharp knife, cut a thin slice of peel and pith from both ends of each orange. Place cut side down on a plate and cut off the peel and pith in strips. Remove any bits of remaining pith. Cut out each segment leaving the membrane behind. Squeeze the remaining juice from the membrane.

4 Mix together the orange segments and juice, the apples and sugar in the pie dish. Place a pie funnel in the centre of the dish. Dampen the pastry strip on the rim of the dish and cover with the pastry. Press the edges to the pastry strip.

5 Brush the top with beaten egg to glaze. Bake for 35 minutes, or until golden. Sprinkle with caster sugar before serving.

Apple Pie Energy 364Kcal/1528kJ; Protein 3.5g; Carbohydrate 46.6g, of which sugars 22.3g; Fat 19.6g, of which saturates 10.7g; Cholesterol 39mg; Calcium 58mg; Fibre 2.8g; Sodium 344mg.
Apple & Orange Pie Energy 444Kcal/1865kJ; Protein 5.7g; Carbohydrate 61.2g, of which sugars 26.3g; Fat 21.4g, of which saturates 13.1g; Cholesterol 53mg; Calcium 108mg; Fibre 5.2g; Sodium 324mg.

Index